POPCORN KING

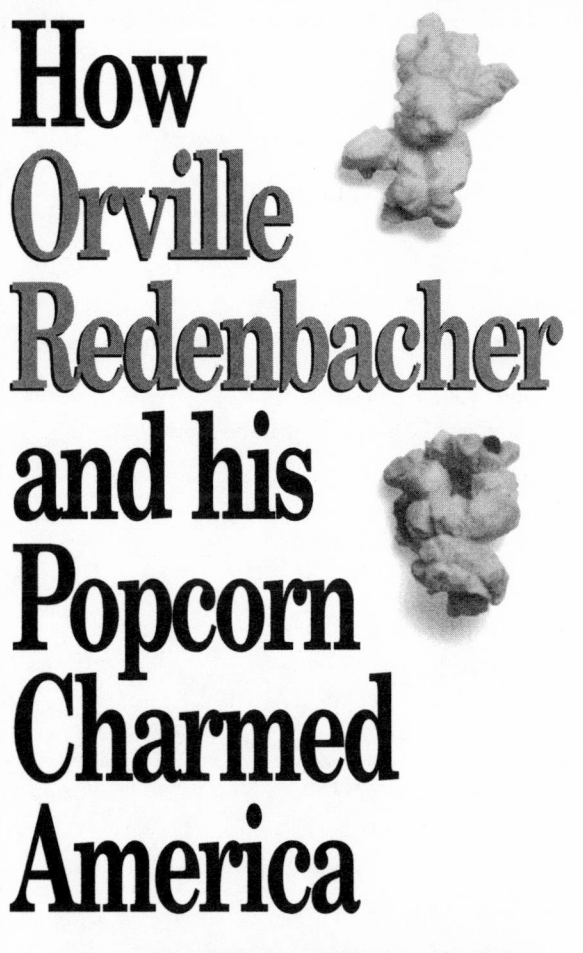

PopcornKing

How Orville Redenbacher and his Popcorn Charmed America

BY LEN SHERMAN

THE SUMMIT PUBLISHING GROUP • ARLINGTON, TEXAS

The Summit Publishing Group
One Arlington Centre, 1112 East Copeland Road, Fifth Floor
Arlington, Texas 76011

Printed in the United States of America.

00 99 98 97 96   010   5 4 3 2 1

Library of Congress Cataloging-in-Publication Data

ISBN 1-56530-222-2
Cover and book design by David Sims

Do one thing and do it better than anyone.

—Orville Redenbacher

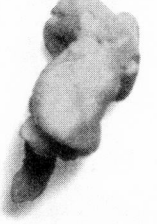
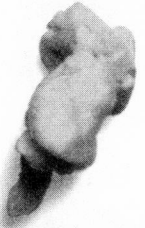

Contents

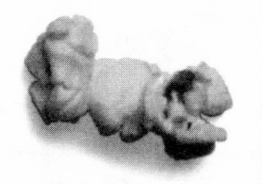

Foreword

Soon after I started working with Grandpa to promote the popcorn, it became apparent that people were fascinated and enamored with him. I was quickly viewed as the source to all of Grandpa's great secrets, regularly being peppered with all manner of question regarding his life, success, and persona. And it was true I knew many of Grandpa's secrets, but they probably weren't the ones the public was looking for. The ones they were looking for didn't exist.

Grandpa had no great secret to success. When pressed for that secret, at first, Grandpa rarely gave the same response twice. Pretty soon, he developed a couple of stock answers. (But this is necessary when you're in the public eye, because most people are interested in about the same things so one gets the same questions many times over. It's exceedingly difficult to find an original answer time and again, so celebrities tend to develop stock answers that are comfortable and well received.) But the truth was, Grandpa knew that his celebrity was in large part an accident.

There are those who will tell you that all hope for celebrity rests on luck. But just because one is in the right place at the right time, so as to achieve at the magnitude of an Orville Redenbacher, doesn't mean that everyone will be able to follow up on that opportunity. Grandpa was prepared to run with the opportunities that presented themselves. And this, perhaps, was his one and only great secret. He was prepared.

Grandpa was innately prepared for the celebrity that found him late in life. He was a tireless worker, maddeningly persistent, educated, witty, and, perhaps, just eccentric enough in his dress to keep someone's passing interest. He was also always looking at long-term goals. In fact, he often forsook pressing items at the expense of tasks that needn't be tended to for years. Many of us reflected that he was lucky enough to get a pragmatist for a partner, Charlie Bowman, when he went into business in the early fifties. I believe both Charlie and Grandpa would admit that Charlie kept the company running on a daily basis and Grandpa supplied the vision for the future.

I mentioned that Grandpa was a tireless worker. The effort that was required to come up with the gourmet hybrid was enough work for anyone's lifetime. Those who have ever tried to hybridize a rose, or any other plant, know that it's just a matter of dogged determination and time. I tell people to imagine that they are in a football stadium full of fans. Imagine that each fan is a stalk of corn. Your job is to go to each cornstalk in the stands and individually pollinate each one. But since the average football stadium only holds about fifty-thousand people, you'll need to do three stadiums before you've pollinated as many cornstalks as Grandpa did each year. True, he hired some help, but he also had to track the results from all those hybridizations. This intense effort began in 1951 when he bought Chester, Inc. and continued even after he had the breakthrough with the Gourmet hybrid in 1965. Through all these tens of thousands of hybrids, Grandpa never lost sight of his goal: To produce a better popcorn. Although he always expected that people would pay for a high-quality corn, he never imagined that he or his popcorn would capture the American fancy the way it did.

Celebrities are elevated to almost mythic heights and I would be less than honest to say that Grandpa didn't enjoy this. But for his part, he was nearly always willing to greet the next person and say a word or two. Indeed, it was often difficult to go anywhere with Grandpa because he had to greet everybody in the crowd. At a food show some years back, Grandpa wandered into the international food section. We don't have a large presence overseas and most of the vendors had never heard of popcorn, much less Orville Redenbacher. This didn't deter Grandpa. He pushed through the crowd and resolutely pressed stickers into puzzled hands that proclaimed, "I met Orville Redenbacher, the Popcorn King."

I had a wonderful relationship with Grandpa and, in trying to capture his essence in this foreword, I'm torn between the grandfather I knew and the grandfather who appeared on the screen. In many respects they were one and the same, but in others a chasm separated these two manifestations. I'm uncomfortable having Grandpa presented as a mythic figure. He had foibles, just like you and me. And he had virtues that cannot be perceived in the fifteen and thirty second ads we made. It would be best to tell you of the grandfather I knew, foibles and all, not just the man in the bow tie with the amusing commercials and great popcorn. But just as his humanity cannot be captured in a television commercial neither can it be captured in this brief writing.

I thank Grandpa nearly every day for that phone call so many years ago when he said, "Gary, you can never know what life is going to bring." He was referring to his own good fortune in achieving success, but more than this I knew he was alluding to something that was to happen to me. Less than a month later, Grandpa's advertising agency asked if I would like to join him in promoting the popcorn. His were shoes that couldn't be filled, but I hope he was proud of the effort. The popcorn created my great opportunity and I tried to run with it the way I thought he would run with it. And for a few brief years I had an inkling of what it was like to be Orville Redenbacher, the Popcorn King. But I prefer to know him as Orville Redenbacher, the Grandfather. Maybe this book will give you some knowledge of both.

—Gary Redenbacher

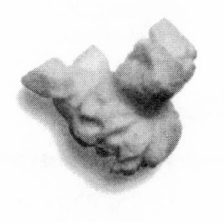

Prologue: Stories and Symbols, Destiny and Dreams, Orville and Popcorn

This book will refute the rumors that Orville Redenbacher sprang whole from Adam's other extra rib; was the firstborn spawn of Zeus and a beautiful, mortal farm girl; or was summoned to earth from his home in the constellations by ancient Egyptian mystics. It will tell an even more extraordinary story, the true story of a man who grew up on a small farm in a small town in Indiana and labored to create the finest popcorn humanity has ever seen. And then this man took his life's work and sallied forth onto the world's stage and told anyone who would listen about his wondrous popcorn. And there is so much to tell.

There are stories about how Orville came to love and understand popcorn, understand it as no human being before him ever has. There are stories about the magnificent, amazing crop itself, about its notable past in communities throughout the world. There are stories about how popcorn is cultivated and changed, and its many applications. There are stories about how Orville became a public person, a public personality, a celebrity. There are stories about popcorn's impact on our diets and our culture.

In a society infatuated with fame and saturated with new sensations, new faces, and new ideas, it is easy to see how Orville Redenbacher could easily be transformed into a mythical figure—perhaps not the progeny of Zeus, but the child of the modern media. In fact, we can imagine that fifty years from today, Americans might believe that that familiar face and smile and black glasses and bow tie on the box or jar (or however popcorn is packaged in the future) is nothing more than a corporate symbol, a contrived, useful character, no more tangible than Aunt Jemima. That is what can happen when reality fades into memory.

So perhaps someday in a distant tomorrow, someone will pick up this book from some neglected corner of a forgotten library, brush off the dust, and turn the pages to discover that Orville Redenbacher once lived, worked, and built an idea into a product and a company that became known throughout the U.S. And that the truth of his life and his work and his accomplishments is more interesting than any fictional accounting devised by an advertising agency or publicity department.

Orville Redenbacher was a man who left a legacy that is both personal and professional. He left behind a food—he left behind an improved food—for all to enjoy, and a family who loved him. He was great at his office and in his fields, but he was even more valuable, more important, and more endearing as a person dealing with his family and friends, business associates, customers, and strangers.

Orville Redenbacher was a man worth knowing, a man who left this world a little better and a little brighter for his having lived in it.

As I said: There is so much to tell.

So let us begin.

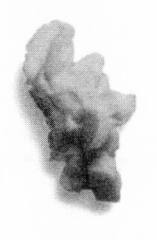

Acknowledgments

To Robert Topping, whose outstanding manuscript and research were an invaluable source of information about the particulars of Orville's life.

This book also would not have been possible without the determined efforts of both Hunt-Wesson, Inc. and Edelman Public Relations Worldwide.

Lesson: The Pop in Popcorn

All right. Before we get to the many matters we're going to discuss—popcorn pedigree, marketing savvy, national television, the American work ethic, Aztec ritual, and, of course, the man himself—we should get one thing straight, one issue out in the open, one subject clear between us before we move along, so there will be no misunderstanding. And that matter, that subject, strikes to the heart, or, more appropriately, the kernel, of everything that will follow. Hence, the essential query: What gives popcorn its kick? Why does this little round shell of grain erupt?

In four words: What makes popcorn pop?

Okay. Very good question.

The correct, more formal name for popcorn is popping corn. In fact, all the manifestations of corn, including popcorn, are actually members of the family of grasses, grasses that produce cereal grains.

You read that right…grass.

As if that's not sufficiently disconcerting, consider that the popcorn plant is a bisexual, single-stalk vegetable composed mainly of carbohydrates. To be exceedingly specific, popcorn is comprised of

71 percent carbohydrate, mainly starch, about 10.5 percent protein, 3 percent fat, and the rest water, with a dash of mineral water thrown in—mineral water being different from regular water in that, well, the former is just chock-full of all sorts of minerals.

The water is the key component in the entire popping process. The water is stored in the endosperm, which is the small circle of soft starch found inside each kernel. As the kernel is heated, so is the trapped water. Heated water quickly becomes steam, which means the H_2O molecules are rapidly expanding, using up all available space inside the kernel. The pressure inside that poor kernel becomes increasingly tough for the outer shell (the hull, which is composed of hard starch and called the pericarp by botanists) to take. Inevitably, the hull cannot stand it any longer and collapses. When it collapses, the water expands even further and the kernel explodes. When the kernel explodes, the soft starch bursts forth and leaps out. The entire kernel turns inside out, and the corn—you guessed it—has popped.

So now you know.

On the other hand, some Indian tribes had their own ideas on the matter. They believed that a tiny demon lived inside each kernel quietly minding his own supernatural business. The demon was content within his secure, little house, quite immune to the distractions and irritations of our everyday world...except for heat. The demon hated heat, and when that heat started to build up outside his little house, he got madder and madder. Eventually, the demon got so mad that he blew his top and blew apart his house, unintentionally begetting a piece of popcorn.

Actually, it's amazing any of those Indians ever wanted to bite into a piece of popcorn.

Consider it popcorn's version of evolutionism versus creationism.

A Pop Star is Born

Orville Redenbacher spent his birthday with David Letterman, not to mention millions of Americans.

"Ladies and gentlemen," announced Letterman, "please welcome the popcorn king!"

On July 16, 1992, Orville Redenbacher walked out onto the stage at the NBC Studios in Rockefeller Center in New York City, home of *Late Night With David Letterman*. The audience cheered and applauded as Orville briskly strode toward Dave. Orville was attired in his trademark bow tie, a red one in this instance, adorned with white popcorn kernels stitched upon the cloth, set off against a white shirt and brown suit.

The two men shook hands and took their seats.

"Welcome to the program," Dave said.

"Thank-you, Dave," Orville said.

"First of all, I'm told that today is your birthday. Is that correct?" Dave asked.

"That's right," Orville said.

"Happy birthday, Orville," Dave said.

The audience fairly erupted in applause and Orville spoke over the din, stating that he was eighty-five years old. The cheering was so loud that Letterman didn't hear Orville, so he asked how old he was.

"I told you," Orville replied with a touch of good-natured bite to his words, "eighty-five years."

"Eighty-five years," exclaimed an impressed Dave. "My God!"

"They planned a big birthday party for me back in Coronado, California," said Orville, "but I didn't think anything could be greater than having a birthday party with David Letterman."

Once again, the audience cheered, as it had cheered for Orville on so many occasions, in so many venues, for so many years.

None of this was all that new to Orville. He was used to the conversational flow of television, and was a renowned expert on the small talk and little jests that constituted the only forms of accepted currency on the talk show circuit. Orville was seen on TV, heard on the radio, and interviewed for the newspapers. When he wasn't in the room, he was talked about, written about, even gossiped about.

It was insane. It was unbelievable. It was obvious, unstoppable, inescapable—at least once it happened.

It was part marketing, part timing, part good fortune—and all Orville. Something about him touched a chord in people. Something about him made men and women and children too, young and old like him. It was that simple: People liked him. Orville's sincerity, honesty, integrity, and his dedication to his popcorn and to his concept came across loud and clear, even bouncing off a satellite and streaking in through a cathode-ray tube.

Once the marketing bandwagon started, it kept picking up speed. Orville was a star, but hardly of the usual variety, and surely never the sort of celebrity—the really difficult and the truly eccentric—the media tend to promote. (Although some might consider devoting one's life to developing the perfect popcorn eccentric, the proof is in the pop.) In short, Orville was a different type of celebrity.

And so Orville was more than a star; he effortlessly, unconsciously embodied much of what we want to believe about ourselves and the American experience. At the same time, he was also a logo and a product. His face was as familiar as a neighbor's and his name a catchword, and thus Orville Redenbacher became an integral part of the national landscape. Here are a few examples, all within a few months of each other:

- In San Diego, the local paper reported that Orville was one of the highlights of a tour bus that visitors took to see the city's most popular sites. The bus drove past Old Town, La Jolla, and Balboa Park, while the cheerful guide explained the area to the wide-eyed tourists, and pointed out the many international stars' houses in the neighborhood: Tom Selleck in Rancho Santa Fe, Raquel Welch in La Jolla, and Orville Redenbacher in Coronado…

- In Washington, D.C., when the Indiana Society threw an inaugural party for more than two thousand Hoosiers, in honor of its favorite son and new vice president, Dan Quayle, the guests received a gift bag filled with goodies including a bottle of Seagram's gin, a Johnny Mathis tape, and a package of Orville Redenbacher's® Gourmet® microwave popcorn.

- In Chicago, when Senator Paul Simon of Illinois ran for president in 1988, his bow tie and Midwest manner caused analysts of repute to comment that the senator's fashion sense—bow ties, eyeglasses, a definite cranial resemblance, and a flat, straight-on speaking manner that was somehow charming with Orville and deadly dull with Simon—rendered him the political version of Orville Redenbacher. Of course, Simon didn't win but no one fixed his Orville resemblance on his defeat.

- In Hollywood, on the long-running TV show *Who's The Boss?*, a character brought a bowl of popcorn into the living room and the very particular Mona (played by Katherine Helmond) naturally asked, "Is this Orville Redenbacher?"

- In San Francisco, at a convention of celebrity look-alikes there was a fake Whoopi Goldberg, an ersatz Bruce Willis, and even a dog posing as beer spokes-beast Spuds MacKenzie, and, yes indeed, a pseudo Elvis standing beside a surrogate Orville Redenbacher.
- In West Lafayette, Indiana, Orville received an honorary degree of agriculture from Purdue University, his alma mater, honoring his more than forty years of popcorn research.
- In Valparaiso, Indiana, the four delegates from the People's Republic of China listened politely as they were escorted around an Indiana college campus by the dean of the business school. The four men comprehended very little English, and they had no reaction as their interpreter translated what the dean had to say about giant corporations such as USX, LTV, and Bethlehem Steel. Then the dean mentioned that Valparaiso was the home of the Orville Redenbacher popcorn company.

The Chinese men paused. "Ah," said Xie Ting-fan, vice president of Hangzhou University in the Zhejiang Province. "Popcorn."

The other Chinese guests smiled and nodded their heads.

Individually, none of these incidents meant very much. But combined they constructed a relief map that showed Orville's singular impact on the cultural scene.

～

Of course, his success was not accidental. Every detail had been planned from choosing a name for the product, to a spokesman, to writing and producing TV commercials and newspaper ads, step by step, dollar by dollar. It had been planned well, but planning could only take it so far. The step beyond, that indefinable quality that captures the public's attention and then the public's affection can't be planned or programmed or forced (it was Orville's own).

Orville was catapulted into the ranks of valued media guests, the modern equivalent to an esteemed social status. It could be said with absolute certainty that Orville hadn't sought celebrity and didn't value it much, but it was good for business.

Lesson: The Inner Works

We've discussed what makes popcorn pop. Now it's high time we talk about what that popping corn is all about. In other words, what is it?

The formal, scientific, Latin name is *Zea mays everta*. That probably has some special meaning for scientists, but I really don't have anything more to say on the subject.

Earlier on, we listed popcorn's ingredients: a lot of starch, a bit of protein, a touch of fat, and a dose of water. But there's so much more to the popcorn story.

As was previously stated, popcorn, same as all corns, is actually a cereal grain, which makes it a member of the family of grasses, as strange as that sounds, evolving from the wild grasses that stretched across the continents at a time when the dinosaurs ruled the earth.

The word "corn" means different things in different places and has been used as the leading cereal crop in any particular region. Thus, while in England corn means wheat, in Scotland we're talking about oats, and in the Bible, the corn stored in the Egyptian pyramids was most likely barley.

In any event, corn—and we mean actual, certifiable corn, not wheat or oats or any other pretender—comes in five varieties.

1. The kernels that comprise sweet corn are higher in sugar content
   than the kernels of any other corn, and thus, they really are
   sweeter. We know it as corn-on-the-cob, and we all love its ten-
   der, luscious taste.
2. Flint corn, often called Indian corn, is that multicolored corn
   hung from front doors and windows and other public places in
   order to provide a festive touch during the holiday season. It
   might be nice to look at with its blue, red, yellow, and black kernels, but it's basically inedible, so just keep looking.
3. Dent corn is grown as livestock feed, which accounts for its other
   names of cow corn and field corn. Aside from a dent on the
   crown of the kernel, dent corn resembles sweet corn, but it has a
   toughness and taste that only a cow could appreciate. More dent
   corn is harvested than any other type of corn, both in the U.S.
   and in Europe.
4. Pod corn is the one corn that looks the most different from all the
   rest. Each kernel is covered by a small, separate husk, which
   makes it pretty in a floral arrangement but lousy to cook and eat.
   That's why you'll inevitably find pod corn, frequently dried out,
   sitting in a basket of flowers.
5. And then there is popcorn. Popcorn grows in a rainbow kaleido-
   scope of colors, though the most common shades are yellow and
   white. Some people prefer one to the other, but the truth is that
   all popcorn is white once it's popped, because the starch inside is
   always white and that's what emerges once the kernel explodes
   and turns inside out. Besides, all the popcorn colors taste the
   same, so it's not much of an issue.

Still, thousands of popcorns can be uncovered, short and tall, round
and thin, from dynamite popcorn with stalks eight feet tall, to
strawberry popcorn with blushing red kernels covering a squat
body. But despite all those countless popcorns, a mere four dozen
or so are judged tasty enough to eat.

The bisexual popcorn stalk is comprised of the tassel at the top, which is male, and the silks that protrude from the ear shoot on the side of the plant, which are female. The tassel sheds thousands of grains of pollen. Some of this pollen is dispersed by the wind, while other grains fall and land on the silks. Each silk is attached to an ovary on the corn's cob. Every time a single grain of pollen lands on a single silk, that grain immediately commences to grow down to the ovary, where it in turn starts propagating a kernel of popcorn.

One grain of pollen, one strand of silk, one kernel of popcorn. Plant bisexual reproduction might have been around for thousands of years, but nobody ever said it was easy.

When popcorn fulfills its destiny and pops, it emerges in one of two shapes: mushroom or snowflake. The former is round and smaller than the latter, which is like a large and puffy cumulus cloud.

And you know those kernels that refuse to pop? In the business, they're called "old maids." The kernels simply don't have sufficient water left inside them to produce enough steam to expand the hull walls and erupt.

Later in life, Orville took to referring to old maids as "shy fellows." He made the change after he discussed the old maid concept on a television show and afterward received angry letters and phone calls from a whole bunch of irate senior citizens.

The truth is, you won't find many old maids in popcorn sold in stores today; especially if your popcorn of choice is Orville Redenbacher's Gourmet popping corn, which boasts an almost perfect popping rate.

Popcorn is a singularly hardy living thing with the ability to survive in rugged terrain and varied temperatures. As has been noted, individual kernels have not only endured for a thousand years, but have popped up nice and firm. Botanists and other scientists are studying popcorn to understand what makes it so hardy, and whether those traits can be passed on to other plants and used to help feed the entire planet.

Stalwart and indomitable, and yet adaptable and multitalented: Could any food claim to be more American than the noble popcorn?

Orville Pops Onto the Scene

Orville's long journey to agricultural acclaim and popcorn prominence, and the attendant fame and fortune, began in the modest family home in Jackson Township, a few miles south of Brazil, the county seat of Clay County in west central Indiana.

Orville's parents, Will and Julia, already had two daughters and a son when their last-born arrived in 1907. Will was a smart farmer and a handy mechanic, and the entire family worked ceaselessly on their farm, which grew over the years from eighty acres to more than two hundred acres. Will had chosen his stake well, for Clay County lies atop the overlap of two important geological riches, exceptionally fertile soil and a deep strata of bituminous coal.

The new baby was named after Orville Wright, who piloted man's first plane at Kitty Hawk, North Carolina, in 1903, and who had enthralled Will Redenbacher with the historic accomplishment.

Orville quickly learned what life was primarily about on the farm: family and work. Orville and his older siblings—Elsie, eleven years older, Karl, seven years older, and Mabel, five years older—had seemingly endless chores to occupy their time. The children would rise before dawn and commence the day by trudging to the barn by the light of kerosene lamps—frequently on fiercely cold Midwestern mornings, literally risking frostbite as they bare-handedly milked the cows. The routine was repeated after the sun went down, when it was just as dark and just as cold.

As Orville got older, his responsibilities became more substantial. For instance: By the age of ten he was tending the straw blower on the threshing rig during harvest.

A seminal event occurred in Orville's life when he was twelve years old for it was then that the boy farmer began to raise his own popping corn. Again, this was no nonchalant effort but a determined enterprise. Orville tended his garden and reaped the harvest, selling it on the cob in fifty-pound sacks to stores in nearby Brazil and Terre Haute. Sales started at a mere ten to $50 a month, but his persistence literally paid off and his popcorn transactions eventually grossed him as much as $150 monthly. The popcorn profits were his to disperse as he chose, and Orville used some for spending money, while putting the rest away for college.

The very idea of going to college was hardly cut-and-dry in Indiana in the first decades of the twentieth century. Until 1920, the year after Orville completed the eighth grade, Indiana had no law requiring children to attend school to the age of sixteen. Orville's parents had stopped their own schooling in the sixth grade. Orville's brother and two sisters were unable to go to high school. Mabel, the younger sister, was so eager to continue her education that she repeated the eighth grade. But the family simply could not afford to send their girls to high school.

Orville selected Brazil High School over a much closer rival because Brazil had a vocational agriculture course. Brazil also meant a daily fourteen-mile round trip. Orville's mom was proud of his achievement; his dad was not quite sure about it; and his grandfather, who had quit after the second grade but was fluent in English and German, was absolutely dismissive.

"That boy," his grandfather once said in exasperation, "will never amount to anything."

Orville was a proud member of the 4-H club and adopted as his hero Horace Abbott, Clay County's first agricultural agent, whose job included supervising all 4-H activity in the county. Abbott possessed the sort of intelligence, enthusiasm, and charisma that made Orville decide that he wanted to follow in his mentor's footsteps and someday himself assume the post of agricultural agent.

Concurrently, Orville was a member of the Clay County 4-H state champion poultry-judging, egg-judging, and corn-judging teams. The next year Orville was part of the county's dairy-judging team that won the state championship at the Indiana State Farm. The team advanced to the national competition in Syracuse, New York. Clay County placed seventh among the state teams, but Orville won second place in the individual competition.

After graduating with honors from high school in 1924, Orville moved on to Purdue University, the Indiana land-grant college located in Tippecanoe County, about sixty miles northwest of Indianapolis. Orville had been such an impressive student that he had received an appointment to the U.S. Military Academy at West Point; however, his heart had long been set on Purdue and its prestigious School of Agriculture.

By forgoing the West Point opportunity, as Orville noted in later years, "I probably missed out on some pretty good wars."

Regardless, his Purdue career was studded with success. He joined the Big Ten school's famed "All-American Marching Band" as a sousaphone player, where, as he endlessly quipped to seemingly every reporter and TV talk show host in America through the years, "I learned to toot my own horn." Orville's other favorite motto arose from his participation on the Purdue track team. In a theme that echoed through his life, Orville wasn't especially fast but he was persistent and hardworking, and he won his varsity letter in his senior year. Orval Martin, a fraternity brother, roommate, and fellow track athlete, recalled that as far as running style was concerned, Orville was "a plodder."

The motto came into play during a meet when Orville was running the mile and kept glancing back to see if the competition was catching up. Finally, a Purdue coach shouted at him, "For God's sake, Reddy, keep running and stop looking around!" A quip was instantly born—"Once you're ahead, keep running and stay ahead."

Orville joined the Alpha Gamma Rho fraternity and was elected to the post of chapter president in his senior year. Perhaps one factor in his election was his superlative ability in the dinner-table contest called "pie-flipping," where the object was to flip your piece of pie as close as possible to the ceiling without hitting it. It must have been a sight to inspire new pledges—Orville, chapter president, attired in his customary bow tie and black glasses, seated at the head of the table, flipping pie after pie.

It wasn't all fun and games, let alone classes and studying, at Purdue. The cost for a school year of two semesters at the state university, from tuition to room and board to expenses, amounted to a little less than $700, which to Orville was a formidable sum. So Orville did what he had to do to get by, which meant taking on a series of jobs. He cleaned Purdue hoghouses and fed chickens at the poultry farm. He worked for a year at the cattle farm, arriving at four each morning to feed the cows a special, experimental diet. He forfeited his Christmas vacation in his junior year to delouse chickens, which entailed catching the uncooperative creatures one by one and dousing them with sodium fluoride. On weekends, for thirty-five cents an hour, Orville and a couple of fraternity brothers returned to the hog farm, where the pigs were used as guinea pigs. The boys had to nab a pig, scrape the blood and dirt from the metal tag in its ear, weigh the beast, put it back in its pen, and start with the next one. Utilizing other talents, he wrote news stories for the agricultural information office.

Somehow, Orville still found time to edit the student newspaper, do the same for the senior yearbook, participate in the 4-H club, and, of course, play in the band and run his fraternity.

And then, not incidentally, there was school. Orville did well in his classes, focusing on agricultural studies. He had nurtured a special interest in plant breeding and genetics since his own popcorn planting days. By the time he reached college, Orville had already contemplated ways of improving popcorn for a surprising number of years. As he told an interviewer on the nationally syndicated television show *PM Magazine* about a simple experiment he had conducted as a young boy: "I collected all the different brands that I could, tin cans or cardboard treated with paraffin, to protect them, so you couldn't see the corn. So one night we opened up eleven different brands and popped them. And some of them were almost junk. And that's when I decided that someone ought to have a better brand of popcorn on the market."

Orville was in the right place for such notions. Two faculty members were on the same popcorn wavelength as Orville, and exciting work was progressing at full speed.

Arthur Brunson was a hybrid corn seed specialist at Kansas State University. While his primary work was with hybrid dent (field) seed corn, he also probed with popcorn. Kansas State refused to fund this latter area of exploration because popcorn was not an important enough cash crop. This negative reaction prompted Brunson to pack up his theories and test tubes and move to Purdue. George Christie, in charge of the Agricultural Experiment Station at the university, welcomed Brunson and his work with open arms, and Purdue quickly established itself as the principal research institute for popcorn in the U.S. Orville liked to hang around the research buildings and glean whatever new information or new ideas he could.

In June 1928, Orville received his bachelor of science degree in agriculture. He was not yet twenty-one and he was ready to take on the world.

Orville's boyhood home that burned down in 1928, his senior year at Purdue University.

Orville's mother and father, Julia and Will Redenbacher.

Orville at age nine, on right, 1916.

Orville covered in 4-H ribbons he had won in various events.

In 1923, Orville played the sousaphone in the Purdue Marching Band.

The 1924 Indiana State Champion dairy judging team for the National Dairy Show included (left to right) Orville, Roy Zenor, Albert Acree, and John Baker.

By 1927, he was the associate editor of the Purdue University yearbook.

In 1928, at Purdue University, Orville was a member of the track team and participated in track and cross-country events.

Young and in love—Orville and Corinne.

Photograph courtesy of Orville Redenbacher's estate.

Following graduation from college, Orville (seated far right) taught at Fontanet High School in the late twenties.

Julia and Will Redenbacher with their children (left to right) Mabel, Karl, Elsie, and Orville.

During the Christmas holidays of 1953, Orville visits with grandson Kevin Fish.

During a trip to Canada, Orville found a great fishing spot.

Corinne and Orville sightseeing in Egypt. c 1968

Orville toured the Great Wall of China.

Orville with tribesmen in Africa. c 1968.

First "People-to-People"
tour of Russia in 1962
included Orville, far right.

As a county agent in Terre Haute, Orville worked with farmers throughout the area.

The Redenbacher family at Princeton Farms. c 1940s.

The photo of himself and Nina that Orville kept in a frame on his desk.

In 1992, Orville with his grandchildren...

...and, with his great-grandchildren.

Lesson: Popping Back to the Past

We'll pause for a historical interlude, and grant a peek into popcorn's past, or at least how that past related to humanity.

Dawn emerged slowly over the magnificent city of Tenochtitlán, the island capital of the Aztec Empire. The city, built on marshy land and surrounded by lakes and floating gardens, set deep in the Valley of Mexico (which would one day emerge anew as the capital of modern Mexico and be known as Mexico City) was one of the great cities of the ancient world. And yet, in the midst of this extraordinary culture, in the center of this remarkable empire, waited an even older city within this ancient city, with an equally remarkable and equally fearsome legacy.

This more ancient city was already a deserted ruin when the Aztecs first came to the Valley of Mexico in the year A.D. 1195, seeking a new home, ready to construct a new kingdom. The new arrivals were awed by what they found, on higher and firmer ground. They discovered the heart of a civilization that had flourished for thousands of years, a metropolis which had been home to perhaps one million people, and had rivaled in power and reach any of the illustrious empires found anywhere in the old world.

The Aztecs called the city Teotihuacán, which many scholars believe means Place Where Men Become Gods. A sacred complex of buildings occupied the heart of Teotihuacán. A tremendous avenue ran down the middle of the complex named Way of the Dead. At one end of the avenue stood the Pyramid of the Sun, a structure of clay and rubble, faced with stone, maybe four times larger than the pyramid of Cheops in Egypt.

The Aztecs revered the mysterious ruins of Teotihuacán and adopted the sacred site as their own. And so we come to the kernel of our tale, the reason for our digression into the Aztec heritage.

Maize was the most important agricultural product in the Aztec community. In fact, maize, or corn, and, quite specifically, the popcorn variety, was so vital to the Aztecs that it actually transcended food and was also used as decoration, as jewelry. Women wore popcorn as necklaces and as ornaments in ceremonial headdresses.

Among popcorn's most important functions was to facilitate the Aztecs' relationship to their deities. You see, the Aztecs worshiped many gods, and depended upon them for sustenance and protection in every aspect of life.

The Spanish, who arrived in Mexico in 1519 under the leadership of Cortés, had never seen popcorn before and were more than a little intrigued. Their many surviving accounts tell of popcorn's role in Aztec society and religion. A Spaniard wrote of how in the course of a rite honoring a god who cared for fishermen, the Aztecs "scattered before him also parched corn, called *momochitl*, a kind of corn which bursts when parched and discloses its contents and makes itself look like a very white flower; they said these were hailstones given to the god of water." Another Spaniard told of how in an Aztec ceremony honoring Huitzilopochtli, the god of war, the virgins "placed over their heads, like orange blossoms, garlands of parched maize which they called *mumuchitl*."

But the employment of popcorn certainly did not end with such benign observances as tossing popcorn on the ground. Oh no, not with the Aztecs, who, along with their overwhelming, consuming interest in their gods, believed that sacrifice, particularly human sacrifice, was the primary means of appealing to the gods. Therefore, since maize was their most important agricultural product, the maize spirits and gods had to be appeased. Priests at every significant temple in the land were charged with selecting one young woman to represent their congregation, who would serve as the people's vehicle in this communal offering.

And so it was on this particular dawn over the magnificent city of Tenochtitlán, the sun alighting the Pyramid of the Sun upon the Way of the Dead, that the priests, drugged and intoxicated the selected young woman. The priests then came and danced with her, for this was a happy ceremony, giving thanks for the maize harvest. Suddenly, the dancing ended and the woman was attacked; her blood used to supposedly bring fertility to the land and crops to the nation.

And so the lesson: Don't take popcorn for granted.

Appreciation of popcorn was not limited to the Aztecs. Popcorn had spread across both North and South America by the time Christopher Columbus landed in the West Indies in 1492. Columbus reported that the natives he encountered sold corsages made of popcorn.

Other European explorers, missionaries and settlers, noted the prevalence of popcorn among the Indians. French pathfinders in the Great Lakes region in the early 1600s discovered that the Indians who lived there popped popcorn in a pottery vessel by heating sand beneath it. A continent away, in Peru, a Spaniard wrote that the Indians "toast a certain kind of corn until it burst. They call it *pisancalla*, and they use it as a confection."

In 1621 the Pilgrims arrived late in the year on the coast of the New World, far from their native England, seeking freedom to live their lives as they saw fit. They named the place they landed Plymouth. In the winter they suffered horribly. Half of the colonists died during the course of the first winter, and it is clear that the entire company would have perished if not for the assistance of the Indians.

It was the Indian Samoset, who walked out of the forest and spoke to the Pilgrims in broken English, who introduced the settlers to Squanto. Through the ages, Squanto gained renown as the colonists' great friend and counselor. Samoset also introduced the Pilgrims to Massasoit, the chief of the Wampanoags; and a peace that lasted for almost fifty years was reached between the two peoples.

And it was the Indians who introduced the Pilgrims to popcorn. On the first Thanksgiving, less than a year after the Pilgrims' arrival, popcorn was not to be denied or ignored in that iconic moment in American history. Along with turkey, cranberries, and other delicious victuals that the company enjoyed during its three-day feast, popped corn made its inaugural appearance among the new settlers. Popped corn was brought to the party by Quadequina, the brother of Massasoit, who carried this unfamiliar, enticing treat in a deerskin bag, and soon a new staple was added to the Pilgrims' pantry.

Popcorn was such a hit with the colonists that the Indians frequently brought popcorn to their peace parleys with the English as a gesture of goodwill.

And popcorn kept rolling along. Colonial housewives found the popcorn a delectable meal, right at the start of the day. That's right, breakfast was blessed with popcorn, for the first breakfast cereal eaten by the white man was popped corn, dressed up with cream and sugar. And why not? After all, popcorn is a whole grain. Consider all the other forms cereal has assumed from bits of barley, bran, wheat, and oats not to mention pieces of chocolate and other candies. So, why not popcorn? But cereal wasn't the only unusual configuration popcorn took on; the Iroquois passed along a recipe for popcorn soup.

Popcorn became as American as apple pie, but with substantially fewer calories to suffer for its impressive pedigree.

6

Orville Redenbacher, Young Adult

Orville met Corinne Rosemond Strate when he was a college senior and she was in her final year in high school. In short order, they were a couple and began discussing marriage. The one hitch was that as Orville was preparing to enter the real world, Corinne, also known as Peggy or Crenny, was all set to enter Indiana University as a journalism student.

Orville fashioned something of a solution. His ambition was still to become a county agricultural agent, same as it had been since meeting Horace Abbott, but that was not a position he could attain overnight. He had an offer from Allied Mills of Fort Wayne, and the chance to become a reporter for *The Prairie Farmer*, the most widely read farm journal in the Midwest. But the best opportunity came from the high school in tiny Fontanet, Indiana, northeast of Terre Haute and west of Coal Bluff, that needed somebody to teach vocational agriculture. The teaching position not only paid more than any other job it was only fifteen miles from Brazil, which allowed Orville to commute from his parents' home. The uncontested topper was that Fontanet was a mere one-hour car ride from Bloomington and Indiana University.

Orville ended up teaching not only vocational agriculture but also biology, industrial arts, and seventh- and eighth-grade agriculture. Finally, he organized Fontanet's first 4-H club.

Meanwhile, Orville and Corinne became engaged. Corinne was ready to drop out of Indiana University after her first semester. She was a fine student but was discouraged in her work and, more to the point, was quite homesick.

Three months before they were married, Orville wrote Corinne a letter that told in simple, honest words how he felt about education in general, about his education, but even more, how he felt about himself and his future:

Dearest Corinne:

[You] must have received a zero in French or else a bawling out from your psychology professor from the way your letter sounded...Corinne, I'm very worried that you do not like your schoolwork, but I'm afraid that won't help matters a whole lot. But really, you haven't been there long enough to tell. Why is it that you hate I.U.?...Gee, I can remember when I was [at Purdue]. I got spells when I thought I would quit. But there were three things that kept me going. First, I always wanted my children to know I was a college graduate and I could tell them all of the college yarns about Dad of '28. I don't know whether you believe this, but I've had that one thought ever since I've been in high school and that's what I'm working for now—a name my children will be proud of. I never told this to anyone before and it does sound rather awkward on paper.

Second, I was afraid the people back home would think I couldn't make my grades, or else got kicked out, and [the third reason] was because I told my folks that I was going to college and I've never had nerve enough to back down on any of my promises.

The first two summers I went home with the full intention of quitting, but these other things got to working and every fall found me back at Purdue. Here I've been rambling on about "I, I, I," but Peggy, maybe if you would think of the future and what a college education means, even for only a year, you wouldn't be so downhearted. I suppose you think that when I see you I'll be preaching sermons to you, but really—I won't...

With love,
Reddy

Orville and Corinne were married the day after Christmas in 1928. They moved into a small, four-room house a mile from Fontanet High School that included three acres, a chicken house, and an outhouse. The newlyweds rented the place for $10 a month.

Less than a year later, Horace Abbott transferred from Clay County to Vigo County, which boasted Terre Haute as its leading metropolis. Abbott also received some federal funds with his new position and asked Orville to be his county 4-H club agent. Orville was now a county agent.

That same year, Corinne gave birth to their first daughter, Billie Ann. Billie Ann would be joined in almost two years by her sister Sue, and eight years later by Gail.

In 1932, Horace Abbott announced he was moving on again to become the county agricultural agent for Marion County, Indiana's most populous county, which encompassed Indianapolis. Orville replaced Abbott as the county agent for Vigo County.

Orville occupied this post for nine years (1932 to 1940 inclusive). His job was to encourage and support agriculture in his county in every manner possible. He served during the Great Depression, which hit farmers particularly hard.

County Agent Redenbacher pioneered the use of radio in agricultural extension. He was the first county agent in the nation to broadcast five-minute farm news and crop reports, which he transmitted every noon over Terre Haute radio station WBOW. He continued the practice throughout his government career, eventually expanding the service by broadcasting directly from farms and other germane locales courtesy of the station's mobile unit, which was one of the first in the country.

The radio show was such a success that Orville's innovation was copied throughout America, a practice that continues to this day on radio and television.

Orville worked with everyone and traveled to every nook and cranny of his territory. Glancing at a list of local agricultural organizations he assisted during his tenure is daunting not only in its length but also in its variety. A sample: The Terre Haute Milk Producers Association, Vigo County Beekeepers Association, Terre Haute Fruit and Vegetable Growers Association, Vigo County Agricultural Association, Vigo County Agricultural Conservation Association, and Older Youth Group. Then there was the Rotary Club, Kiwanis Club, chamber of commerce, individual merchants, and, as always, the 4-H Club.

Orville always strove to expand 4-H activity. In 1930, 4-H membership was less than two hundred seventy in his county. In one year, with his first appointment as a county agent, he raised that number to six hundred forty boys and girls. By 1939, Orville had enrolled up to twelve hundred 4-H members.

By his own accounting, in his last year as county agent, Orville logged nearly forty thousand miles within the county, spent three hundred forty days in his office and approximately the same number in the county's farm fields. Forty-five thousand citizens attended an incalculable number of meetings of all kinds, and his individual farm consultations totaled more than sixteen thousand five hundred, and that astounding total did not include more than seven thousand phone calls to his office. In addition, twelve hundred news articles appeared in local newspapers, nearly all of which were generated by his office.

His pride and joy, "his baby"—radio broadcasts—increased excess in number through the years. In 1939, Orville averaged one, sometimes two, broadcasts every day except Sunday, amounting to exactly three hundred forty-four.

For all his work, for all his efforts, for all his good intentions, Orville suffered terrible frustrations. The Great Depression was too deep, brutal, and long. Many people lost everything they had, from their businesses and farms to their homes, hopes, and dreams. Orville did what he could but it was often not enough, because fixing this incredibly huge and complex economic, political, meteorological, social calamity was far beyond the range of the Vigo County agricultural agent.

Orville understood this, but it did not make him feel any better. That was not his nature. Still, he fought the good fight, and won the winnable battles.

All this was to change when Henry and Hy Smith, owners of the Princeton Mining Company, paid Orville a visit. They had purchased the land over their mines and oil wells and needed someone to manage their new property, which consisted of twelve thousand acres. They needed someone like Orville.

Lesson: Popcorn's Serious, Scientific Side

Time flies both forward and backward when discussing the popcorn chronicles, which seems only appropriate because popcorn was there at humanity's beginning and popcorn remains with us still, and now we shall plunge into the furthermost recesses of the human record. To quote Dr. Paul C. Mangelsdorf, professor of botany and head of the Botanical Museum of Harvard University: "There is no doubt that the original corn—wild corn and early cultivated corn—was popcorn, and it is quite probable that the first use which man made of corn was by popping."

The research is considerable, and has been catalogued by the Popcorn Institute, which seems a reasonable place for popcorn cataloguing to be conducted. So with a quick nod to the Popcorn Institute, here are some heavy-duty facts:

- A Zapotec funeral urn found in Mexico, hailing from A.D. 300, delineates a maize god with popcorn both in his headdress and in his hands.
- Popcorn was discovered at Huaca Prieta, on the north coast of Peru, in the course of excavations of the Cupisnique culture, dating from 800 B.C.

- The Mongolion Indians partook in the delights of corn in their villages in Pine Lawn Valley in west central New Mexico, circa A.D. 300 to A.D. 1000.
- On the east coast of Peru, grains of popcorn one thousand years old have been discovered that are so well preserved that they will still pop.
- Speaking of thousand-year-old popcorn, the forerunners of the Pueblo Indians enjoyed our very special grain, as evidenced by a popped kernel located in a cave in southwestern Utah.
- The Incas, rulers of a South American empire that at its height stretched two thousand miles from Ecuador to northwest Argentina, until their defeat and conquest by the Spanish conquistador Pizarro in A.D. 1532, carved small stone ears of corn that are believed to have been actual size reproductions of early popcorn ears.
- And, then there is the Bat Cave. The Bat Cave, located in west central New Mexico, is sort of the Holy Grail of ancient popcorn research, the journey to the center of the popcorn universe. Expeditions uncovered layer after layer of popcorn history.

On the more contemporary end of the scale, popcorn has been found among the artifacts of the San Pedro Phase of the Cochise Indian culture, ranging from approximately 2500 B.C. to A.D. 500. Another layer held popcorn dating back to 2500 B.C. and was attributed to the Chiricachua Phase of the Cochise Indians. But even older popcorn awaited discovery in the cave. Popcorn has been found that ranges in size from smaller than a penny to two inches, and has been shown to be fifty-six hundred years old. That's the sort of information that makes scientists sit up and take note, because it strongly suggests that popcorn originated in North America.

If you ask the Popcorn Institute, headquartered in Chicago, they will provide you with several pages that delineate the scientific ups-and-downs, the ins-and-outs, the whys-and-wherefores of popcorn. I'm talking about the hard stuff, the objective and theoretic core of the matter. And because I know you want to know it all, I'll provide a taste (albeit a dry taste) of some of this down-and-dirty information.

It has been proven that popcorn was the earliest form of maize. In July 1950, the aforementioned Dr. Mangelsdorf wrote an article entitled "The Mystery of Corn" in *Scientific American*, in which he stated:

> U.S. botanist E. Lewis Sturevant, one of corn's most astute investigators, concluded more than half a century ago that primitive corn must have been both a pod corn and a popcorn. Evidence is now accumulating to show that Sturevant was right. In the remains of prehistoric civilizations unearthed in South America, popcorn predominates over other types.
>
> Pottery utensils for popping corn, as well as actual specimens of the popped grains, have been found in prehistoric Peruvian graves. Certainly there is nothing new about the popcorn which modern Americans consume so lavishly as part of the movie going ritual. Popcorn is an ancient food, and it is quite possible that primitive man first discovered the usefulness of corn as a food plant when a wild grain was accidentally exposed to heat. This would have exploded the small, vitreous, glume-covered kernels, and transformed what to people with no grinding tools, other than their own teeth, was a very unpromising food into tender, tasty wholesome morsels.

Dr. Mangelsdorf surfaced again in the October 1958 issue of the *Proceedings Of The American Philosophical Society* explaining that data gained from the Bat Cave popcorn specimens helped him reconstruct this earliest popcorn by hybridizing popcorn with pod corn.

"Although we have not yet completely reconstructed wild corn," wrote Dr. Mangelsdorf, "nor duplicated exactly the most primitive specimens from either Bat Cave or LaPerra Cave," the doctor asserted that they came close and had conclusively demonstrated that the ancestor of all corn, the Adam and Eve of this grassy species, the corn alpha, was a popcorn plant.

Other scientists have supported Mangelsdorf's determination. In 1950, Dr. Hugh Cutler and Dr. Edgar Anderson, both from the Missouri Botanical Garden in St. Louis, published an article in the

Southwestern Journal of Anthropology with the impressive appella-
tion, "Methods of Corn Popping and Their Historical Significance."
In the article, they reported:

> The earliest varieties of maize must certainly have had small
> kernels as hard as glass. How could a primitive fold have uti-
> lized them? Most probably by eating the immature kernels, by
> sprouting the kernels to make a malt beverage, or by popping
> the kernels with heat. Hence the special significance to the stu-
> dent of maize, of fermented maize beverages, of green corn and
> of popcorn.
>
> The occurrences of popcorn at each archaeological site in
> both Mexico and Peru, as well as the actual prehistoric popped
> kernels in the latter area have served to justify this hypothesis.
> The recent discovery of a prehistoric pod corn which was also a
> popcorn, as determined by Mangelsdorf and Smith (1949) at an
> early New Mexican site, shows how long a history must be
> assigned to what we ordinarily look upon as a trivial everyday
> confection.
>
> ...Maize, our most viable cultivated plant, has myriad vari-
> eties clustered in several vaguely defined races. There is a pop-
> corn in each race and in most cases the popcorns seem to be the
> oldest and most sharply defined examples of each race.
>
> ...Like the making of string figures by children, corn popping
> has more significance for the anthropologist than is immediately
> apparent...though we ordinarily associate it with circuses and
> carnivals, it is one of the world's oldest, as well as most distinctive
> goods. It is therefore an important item in the story of mankind.

So consider popcorn as a bond to our primitive past, a clue to who
we were and who we still are, for it is a direct link to our most
ancient ancestors.

So many things have changed and so many haven't. We no longer
grow or harvest popcorn as did our unknown forefathers. We no
longer pop popcorn as did our prehistoric cousins. We no longer
imbue popcorn with the same religious gravity as did our rugged

ancestors. We no longer decorate our bodies and attire with pop-corn as did those who walked the earth before time itself.

But the most crucial thing about popcorn hasn't changed at all: It still tastes the same... in other words, delicious.

8

Orville's Professional Popcorn Saga Begins

Princeton Farms' twelve thousand acres was divided into twenty-four separate tracts situated in three counties, which made it the largest farm in Indiana. The new manager was very satisfied with his contract: home, board, $4,500 a year, and 10 percent of the farm's net profits.

Farming is always a difficult proposition. It is dependent on whether the sun shines or the rain falls, whether nature provides what the soil and plants need when they need it. One year was profitable; the next, the corn, soybeans, and oats planted in the bottomlands were all ruined by flooding too late in the season to replant. All of the farm's profits—including Orville's 10 percent—were wiped out.

Forever the innovator, Orville was one of the first farmers in the state to plant hybrid dent seed corn. Before too long, his hybrid seed corn acreage was the largest in Indiana. Orville's work helped lead Indiana to a position where today hybrid seed corn is a key agricultural product.

In Orville's first year, he invested heavily in the aforementioned hybrid dent seed corn, as well as diversifying the farm's operations to ensure profitability. In 1941, his second year, he moved on to his first love: popcorn. Specifically, Orville planted the hybrid popcorn seed developed in the 1930s by Purdue scientists.

Orville had stayed in close contact with Purdue's agricultural experiment station and the U.S. Department of Agriculture Extension Service, and was well-informed on the latest developments. So when Orville planted his popcorn, he knew just what to do.

He had built a processing plant for the dent corn hybrid seed, and now built another to process hybrid popcorn seed. Orville eventually sold popcorn seed throughout the U.S. and Canada, and then to growers in Hungary, Israel, Columbia, Argentina, Chile, and South Africa.

In 1944, Orville began raising popcorn for the supermarket trade. He also continued to increase his farm's acreage; by 1951, Princeton Farms' operations had grown by 50 percent, now encompassing eighteen thousand acres either owned outright or under contract. Orville first raised a Purdue variety called P32. In 1948, he started to plant one of the popcorn hybrids he had developed, and then processed and sold it in sealed containers under the Princeton Farms label.

Preoccupied as Orville was with popcorn, he gave his all to the farm's other products and commodities. He not only planted wheat, soybeans, and other crops, but also raised premium livestock, including Aberdeen Angus cattle, Guernsey dairy cows, Hampshire hogs, and Hampshire sheep.

At the same time, Orville seized upon another advance in agriculture. In 1949, he purchased a barrel of a new Allied Chemical Company product called Solution 32, or Uran by its brand name. Orville experimented by spraying selected sections of his fields with Uran. He was so impressed with the effect on his crops that he bought the second and third tank car loads Allied Chemical manufactured. To accommodate this huge purchase, Orville built the first farm storage tank for this new product ever constructed in the U.S.

Uran was another name for liquid fertilizer, and Orville's enthusiastic embrace of it made him a millionaire. Thirty years later, when fertilizer prices went through the roof, Orville was the largest distributor in Northern Indiana. Today, liquid fertilizer is in universal use throughout the continent, but it was Orville Redenbacher who at the start grasped its potential, and established himself as the very first person to use and sell it commercially.

But back to popcorn. Popcorn was there at Orville's beginning, just as it was at humanity's beginning; it remained a constant companion through every step of his life.

Whether talking about popcorn or dent corn, the process of hybridization requires hard physical labor. The term for this labor is "detasseling," which refers to the process essential to crossing two varieties of corn so breeders get the best qualities of both.

As previously stated, the tassel is the male part of the stalk, while the silks comprise the female part. The pollen tumbles from the tassel to the silk, where it slinks down to the ovaries and gives birth to a kernel of popcorn.

Thus, to detassel means the removal of the tassels so the corn plants do not pollinate themselves. It is the task of detasselers to go through the fields and, by preselected rows, remove the tassels so the plants receive pollen from a different corn variety in the next row, thereby creating the cross-hybrid seed.

In a field as large as Princeton's that meant an enormous amount of work, which could not be delayed without risk of upsetting the entire hybrid process. There was always a need for more workers to march through the hot fields and detassel, so Orville enlisted the assistance of his children, just as his own father had done.

FORGING A PARTNERSHIP

Orville met Charles Bowman during the 1940s. Charlie was also a Purdue graduate, class of 1941, who had majored in agricultural education. His professional specialty was seed certification, and he became the manager of the Indiana Crop Improvement Association seed certification service, which involved maintaining the quality of the hybrid grain and pasture grass seeds raised and sold by Indiana farmers. Since Orville's operation was one of the state's largest producers of hybrid seed corn and popcorn seed, Charlie had frequent occasion to visit Princeton Farms and the two men became fast friends.

In 1950, Charlie had the opportunity to purchase one of the oldest seed corn companies in Indiana. Charlie phoned his friend Orville. The two men had previously talked about how they could get together and "sell our know-how." That had been idle, dinner chatter—this was for real.

Charlie asked Orville what he thought.

"Well," Orville replied, "I think we ought to look into it."

"Are you serious about this, Orville?" Charlie asked.

That was a reasonable question, because Orville had a well-paying job with lifetime security, and a family that depended on him. In fact, the same was true for Charlie. But this was a challenge and an opportunity, and neither Orville nor Charlie were genetically constituted to let either of those notions just slip away and pass by.

Many years later, in 1987, Orville was asked by an interviewer at a popcorn convention if he had lived by some sort of business philosophy. Since this wasn't exactly a journalistic exercise but an industry showcase, Orville knew the question was coming and was ready with his response.

"My philosophy of business?" repeated Orville. "Well, every once in a while, I write something for a book or a magazine. And I think it's probably best described in something I wrote some time ago, in a salute to America. And if I could just read that last paragraph."

Orville picked up a piece of paper and began to read.

"I've followed the classic homespun principles," he said in his trademark forthright manner. "Never say die. Never be satisfied. Be stubborn. Be persistent. Integrity is a must. Anything worth having is worth striving for with all your might. Does it sound corny? Honestly, that's all there is to it. There is no magic formula."

Though that 1987 interview might have been nothing more than a typical convention setup, designed to promote the industry and its product, Orville's answer was typically honest and clear. That was exactly how he had acted and how he had proceeded almost forty years before when he took the biggest step of his life.

Orville and Charlie had determined to go into business for themselves. Each man put up $10,000 for the down payment, negotiated a small bank loan, and away they went.

Lesson: Inventorying the Tools

It's interesting to note how our ancestors popped their popcorn, since they didn't have a microwave. In accordance with the human condition that we all crawl before we walk, the very first method of popping corn was—yes, you guessed it—tossing popping corn into the fire and waiting for the corn to heat up and the kernels to pop, popping here and there. In fact, human beings probably discovered the reality of popping corn when some fellow accidentally dropped a cob or handful of kernels into a fire, and then presto, popcorn! Of course, we can't be exactly sure why this same fellow decided that this small, exploding whitish thing was suitable for placing inside his mouth, chewing, swallowing, and digesting.

Not that we should be ungrateful, but still, imagine the setting: You're tired after a long day chasing bison or hunting buffalo, and puttering around, doing the household chores. So the fire's blazing away while you lug wood, skins, plants, and vegetables around the place. Every now and then, you drop something—after all, it's dark and you're exhausted. So you're walking and puttering and dropping and then you hear this noise and you turn, half-expecting some wild creature to come streaking out of the night, when you're smacked in the forehead by a tiny projectile. It bounces off you and lands in the dirt, and you pick it up, clean it off, roll it around in your fingers, smell it, think about it, and then decide—Hey, that looks like good eating!

Anyway, it undoubtedly happened something like that, and of course we're all beholden to that adventurous diner.

After that initial experience with popcorn, it probably didn't take too long for men and women to find a better technique than tossing and chasing the popcorn around the campfire. Eventually, many Indians used the simple but effective method of heating sand in the fire, spreading the scorching sand on the ground, mixing in popcorn, and stirring until the popping commenced. Sand was a great improvement over fire because kernels were no longer sacrificed to the flames, thereby cutting down on burnt, inedible kernels.

The Winnebagos of the Great Lakes employed another popping process, as related by Whirling Thunder, one of their chiefs, early in this century. Whirling Thunder spoke of how the members of his tribe popped corn the same way through time immemorial, by inserting a stick through the cob and holding it over the campfire. This extremely direct method caused most of the popped kernels to pop right off the cob, which naturally led to that old problem of finding kernels in every nook and cranny as they flew around the place.

Ratcheting up on the sophistication scale, we find many tribes in both North and South America using special corn popping pots, which fundamentally operated in the same manner modern poppers operate, i.e., a pot, fire, and oil. Constructed of clay or metal, a pot might have a sizable hole on one side, a large handle around the top, and tripod legs. Poppers fifteen hundred years old have been discovered in Peru and Guatemala, adorned with the improvement of a lid to let the steam escape.

The Papago Indians in Arizona do their popping precisely as their ancient ancestors did, in shallow clay vessels, sometimes up to eight feet wide, over an open fire.

In the middle of the seventeenth century, as the Spanish conquered Mexico and South America, a fellow named Falix de Azara took time out to write of a singular sort of popcorn he found in Paraguay, with kernels on the tassel, which when "it is boiled in fat or oil, the grains burst without becoming detached, and there results a superb bouquet fit to adorn a lady's hair at night without anyone knowing what it was. I have often eaten these burst grains and found them to be very good."

Amazing: Whether blown from a fire, plucked from the dirt, or picked out of a woman's hair, popcorn still tastes delicious. How many foods can you say that about?

TOOLS FOR POPPING

The new Americans invented their own popping implements, starting rather basically and quickly improving. In a version of "reinventing the wheel," early colonial poppers were just flattened sheets of iron with a few holes punched through them. The popcorn was placed on the iron sheet, the iron was placed on the fire, and the inevitable would occur, with the popcorn jumping all over the room, just like in the old days with the fire and our first intrepid eater.

The colonists fixed their problem with typical Yankee ingenuity. They perforated the sheet and curled the edges and turned them into devices resembling warming pans. In even more sophisticated fashion, they took a punctured iron sheet and twisted it into a shape reminiscent of a small cage, which revolved on an axle in front of the fireplace, allowing the kernels to tumble around and around, avoiding unequal cooking and burning.

Much later, back in Indiana, young Orville would watch as his parents made their own popcorn. Their method involved a rectangular screen-wire basket with a long handle, which allowed them to shake a large batch of popcorn over the hot coals glowing in the fireplace.

By the time Orville was in college, the electric popping corn popper was on the market, which was a great boost to the whole popcorn industry. After all, it's a lot easier to stick the plug into the wall and wait, rather than stand and shake a long metal pole over an open fire.

First there was the nonautomatic popper, and then the automatic version, the difference being that the latter came equipped with a built-in thermostat that ensured the temperature didn't rise beyond the proper point. Then we have the hot-air poppers, which don't employ any oil at all.

And then there's the microwave, which assuredly and eternally altered the world of popcorn by making the whole popping business so easy, clean, and totally neat, that no sensible person ever has a reason for not popping popcorn.

MOVIE POPCORN

Aside from the individual craft of popping, the other field of endeavor is public popping, those poppers which produce mass quantities of popcorn for sale at movie theaters, candy and specialty stores, and other business venues.

In 1885, Charlie Cretors manufactured peanut roasters, i.e., machines that roasted peanuts. But that was just the beginning for Cretors, for in the year 1893 Cretors invented the automatic popcorn popping machine. Cretors introduced the machine at the Columbian Exposition, during the Chicago World's Fair in 1893. It was a crowd stopper, as people were amused by this steam-powered machine's ability to produce loads of popcorn. Before long, word spread far and wide about Cretors's creation.

Now popcorn was already sold on the street by vendors who utilized wire baskets over open flames. Cretors's machine rapidly became quite the thing for the enterprising storekeeper to post outside his shop, which was partly used as a source of additional revenue but mainly used to attract attention and customers.

As for those individual popcorn vendors, well, they naturally wanted to be as close to the crowds as possible. The crowds were found at city parks and county fairs, and so were the vendors. The crowds were also found outside movie theaters, which was quickly established as the prime popcorn selling site.

To accommodate the vendor, who needed to be mobile to go from location to location, Cretors built poppers that were mounted on wheels, so they could either be pushed by hand or pulled by horses or mounted on wagons or trucks.

Even though the popcorn sold well outside the Nickelodeons, the theater owners, who evidently fancied themselves involved in some refined activity (remember, this was a long time ago) wanted nothing to do with the popping and cracking and thoroughly noisy machines, not to mention the messy popcorn they produced. So they relegated the vendors to down the block, but people kept buying popcorn and sneaking it into the theater.

The theater owners stuck to their irrational ban until the Great Depression struck in the 1930s. Movie attendance faltered but popcorn eating did not. Banks went under, businesses went bust, but popcorn and popcorn vendors thrived. (In fact, times were so tough that some people had popcorn as their main meal because it was good and cheap.)

The theater owners finally got the hint and invited popcorn inside. Many theaters often made more money with their popcorn than with their films. Poppers seized command of the lobby and have ruled ever since. Popcorn is still synonymous with movie theaters.

One last item, definitely classified under the trivia heading: The vendors originally sold popcorn in paper bags. However, butter often leaked from the paper bags onto people's clothing. Vendors introduced buckets, which were stronger and did not leak; and, later, waterproof sacks.

By the way, Cretors still manufactures popcorn machines, with a fourth-generation Charlie at the helm.

Making Popcorn History

Orville and Charlie Bowman had purchased the George F. Chester & Son Seed Company, established in 1936. The Chester company produced hybrid corn and other seeds on a contract basis for several large eastern U.S. seed concerns. The company had recently expanded its physical facilities and had opened a seed store and agricultural chemical business in Valparaiso, Indiana. It was a solid company, with fine prospects.

Nonetheless, both men knew it would take some time before the venture could really be made profitable. They hoped to gross $100,000 in the first year, which wouldn't be enough to support both families. Charlie retained his job for another eighteen months with the Purdue Agricultural Alumni Seed Improvement Association, while Orville devoted himself full-time to the company.

Orville and Corinne took a one-year lease on their first home in Valparaiso and then moved to an apartment for several years. Eventually, they built a large home on the southeast side of Valparaiso in an upper-middle-class area called Coolwood Acres. For many years, the house at 959 Coolwood Drive was the center of the expanding Redenbacher clan. As their daughters married and started families of their own, holidays and summer vacations were reserved for a return to Valparaiso.

Appropriately, Valparaiso is the home of the annual Valparaiso Popcorn Festival, which takes place each September and attracts more than eighty-thousand popcorn lovers. The town has honored Orville and the Redenbacher family for the past seventeen years and has plans to continue the festival for years to come.

As his fortunes improved, Orville had the backyard landscaped into a scene approximating a child's paradise. A waterfall was installed to go along with the series of three pools, along with an arched bridge, lots of lush and varied vegetation, different toys, games, contraptions, and apparatuses. The memories of the grandchildren are rich and many: Grandpa cranking homemade ice cream on hot summer days; Grandma's potter's wheel, where she would give a lesson in "throwing" to all those interested; the kids pulling a ricksha around the block; Grandma's sewing room with its collection of dolls; the basement with the pool table and Ping-Pong table and all sorts of board games; the traditional Easter egg hunt, followed by Grandpa's singular Easter custom, when he would climb onto a stepladder in the middle of the living room and toss dollar bills into the air so they would float to the ground and the grandchildren could scramble for them.

But that was all in the future, for before Valparaiso could become established as the Redenbacher clan's haven, Orville had to make the new company a success.

In 1953, Charlie joined Orville on a full-time basis, and they decided to consolidate and move the entire operation to Valparaiso. They purchased twenty acres east of the city to build the company's office, as well as additional grain and fertilizer facilities. A third partner, G. L. "Jack" Findling, joined the company in 1954 as vice president for seed corn and small grains.

The trio moved rapidly forward. The partners expanded to become the major producer and seller of Kankakee Valley Hybrid seed corn and certified small grain and soybeans in northwest Indiana. They changed the name of the company to Chester Hybrids, Inc., and started to diversify. Chester Hybrids produced liquid fertilizer, application and spray equipment, as well as an engineering service to develop and install grain-drying and grain-handling equipment and systems. The rising demand for liquid fertilizer prompted Chester Hybrids to build a production plant for its new product, KV Liquid Fertilizer.

Of course, nothing could cause Orville to become too distracted from his first passion, the breeding of popcorn.

"Do one thing and do it better than anyone," Orville would tell anyone who would listen. It was one of his favorite sayings, and it was a saying he lived by and proved valid through his unending work with popcorn.

Orville plunged the company into the development and production of hybrid popcorn seed. Chester Hybrids devoted land for a plant nursery at Valparaiso and acquired a small plot near Homestead, Florida, as a winter nursery.

Carl Hartman answered a "help wanted" ad in the *Valparaiso Vidette-Messenger*, in 1959. He was thirty-four years old and a graduate of Iowa State University with a specialty in animal husbandry. He worked for the Chicago Stockyards until he and his wife decided they had had enough of the big city. Ready for a change, Carl sought out a different kind of place, and he found it in Valparaiso. Whatever its virtues, Valparaiso was definitely not Chicago.

Carl started in garden seed sales, but soon found his way into plant breeding. He became an expert at working with different grains. He soon turned his attention to popcorn, working with Orville to improve their seed, which the company sold under the brand name RedBow Popcorn Hybrids. RedBow, created by combining the last names Redenbacher and Bowman, employed a red bow tie as its logo, in honor of Orville's ever present emblem.

On one acre, Carl planted three thousand popcorn plants accounting for eighty-three varieties, assembled from hybrids from both North and South America. He let the wind do the pollinating and arrived at two thousand new crosses. He then selected the best for purity and quality, year after year, and started the process all over again.

In 1965, Carl and Orville achieved a dream that Orville had actively sought for some forty-odd years: Popcorn that was light and fluffy, left hardly any unpopped kernels, possessed minimal hulls, retained an excellent taste, and, finally, met what is the ultimate test in the popcorn world—the forty-four to one ratio in volume of popped to unpopped corn. Stated in plain English, forty-four-to-one means that each cup measure of unpopped kernels will produce forty-four cup measures of popped corn. To demonstrate how difficult and distant that ratio actually was, at the time most popcorn had a popping ratio of less than twenty-five-to-one.

The Chester Hybrids laboratory in Valparaiso held a tall, clear, plastic cylinder calibrated just for that test. Esther Lacy, a Chester Hybrids employee, remembered Orville's response on that day when the latest strain popped its way to attaining the forty-four-to-one mark. "He was like a little kid," she said. "He was laughing and running around the place. He was so elated." Orville could only exclaim three words, which he kept repeating:

"We made it! We made it!"

Orville always gave Carl the credit for this accomplishment. "He did a tremendous job," Orville would say. "It was Carl who developed the hybrid that made Redenbacher a famous name."

Carl did deserve a great deal of the credit, but so did Orville. His dream harkened back to his childhood on the family farm, when he had made popcorn picked from his own patch and popped it on the coal stove on cold winter evenings, as well as selling to grocery stores in Terre Haute in fifty-pound sacks. The dream had taken substance at Purdue, where he studied the experiments of Arthur Brunson at the Agricultural Experiment Station; and then at Princeton Farms, where Orville had incorporated that knowledge in his own cross-breeding efforts. Orville had continued his work alongside Carl, sometimes overseeing the younger man's labors, sometimes spending weeks and months at the Homestead winter plot, planting, pollinating, and detasseling the hybrids himself.

No less than thirty thousand popcorn hybrids were crossed and created in order to find just the right mix, to produce as close to a perfect popcorn as was possible.

Now the work was done. Now the people had to be told—and sold. And though that sounds easy now, given the subsequent extraordinary success of Orville Redenbacher's Gourmet popcorn, it was not. In fact, it was far more difficult and problematic than anyone had imagined. The entire forty-year struggle almost amounted to naught, and this near-perfect popcorn almost disappeared without a trace.

11

Lesson: Yes, Virginia, Popcorn Really is Good for You

Turn on the TV, if you dare, and find out what's bad for you today. You know what I'm talking about—a day's worth of hamburgers contain fewer calories than a single allegedly "low-fat" muffin, keeping your clothes in those plastic sheathes after dry cleaning can cause horribly noxious fumes to leach into your most intimate apparel and result in some sort of terrible disease, you can get tuberculosis from riding in an airplane....

The good news part of the tale is popcorn, because it has not betrayed us. Popcorn was always promoted as being good for us, and nutritionists have only found over time that popcorn is even better for us than we ever thought.

So let's get to the facts, and even though the facts aren't too exciting, at least when compared to the World Series or a movie premiere, the facts are gratifyingly, reassuringly, nutritionally positive.

Let's talk calories, because everybody has an opinion about calories. Popcorn has precious few of them. One cup of air-popped popcorn has about twenty-five calories. Compare that to pretzels at one hundred eleven for that same cup, potato chips at approximately one hundred fifty, and vanilla ice cream at—well, don't even ask—

three hundred forty-nine.

The main function of cereal grains, and that includes popcorn, is to provide the body with heat and energy. Nothing does that better than carbohydrates, and popcorn is loaded with them.

Popcorn doesn't shortchange protein and iron. It also contains calcium, phosphorus, thiamin B_1, riboflavin B_2, and niacin. And let's not forget popcorn's more than respectable fiber content.

Just to prove that all this isn't mere hyperbole, here's a few official sources to ponder. The American Dietetic Association judges popcorn to be an acceptable exchange for bread on weight-control diets—ditto for The American Diabetes Association. The National Cancer Institute recommends popcorn as a "moderately high source of fiber." The American Dental Association includes popcorn on its honor roll of sugar-free foods.

Who could ask for more? Asking or not, there is more, and while it's not about nutrition, it definitely is a benefit. Popcorn is as inexpensive as food comes. It can be purchased for as little as four cents a quart—although not at a movie theater. If you extrapolate that to the average American family of mother, father, and approximately 2.3 children, it adds up to just over seventeen cents a meal.

All hail the mighty and yet modest popcorn!

Frustration and Fame

So Orville had his popcorn, his fabulous popcorn. After so much effort and so many years, the moment had come to share his pride and joy with the world.

Except the world wasn't exactly interested.

Orville's popcorn was perfected in 1965. By that time, Chester, Inc. had undergone many changes, apart from a formal shortening of its name. The dent hybrid seed corn business had been sold off and the company had broadly diversified. Chester, Inc. produced and sold agricultural chemicals, grain bins and corn dryers, commercial buildings, and farm irrigation systems. The company had developed into one of the most prosperous agribusinesses in the Midwest.

Chester, Inc. was also the largest producer of hybrid popping corn seed, which was still sold under the RedBow label. Of the one million pounds of popcorn seed raised in the U.S. each year, Chester, Inc. accounted for 60 percent.

But that was old news, for a new day, and a new popcorn, had arrived.

Popcorn processors had a simple philosophy: cheaper was better. Popcorn was sold by the pound, and the bottom-line price was all that consumers cared about. Orville refused to believe their philosophy. He believed: Give the people a better product and they will beat a path to your door.

But the processors stood firm. Orville's popcorn was significantly more expensive to produce. Its yield per acre was far lower than other commercially grown popcorn seed. Farmers charged Chester, Inc. a $50-per ton premium for raising it; and, in turn, Chester, Inc. insisted that to avoid bruising the kernels, farmers should harvest the popcorn with an ear-corn picker rather than with a combine.

Orville explained the intricacies of ensuring that his perfect popcorn seed stayed exactly that way, from soil to shelf, in an article he wrote not long after his popcorn finally started to gain public acclaim:

> In October, the moisture content of popcorn kernels concentrates down to about nineteen percent. That's the point when the harvest begins, because the proper moisture content is vital to corn that will pop to your satisfaction.
>
> Modern corn-harvesting combine machinery would bruise some of my kernels. Bruised kernels will not pop with quality, so I use only special harvesting equipment that harvests the corn on the ear. This is more expensive but it ensures top quality.
>
> Next the shucked ears are held in bins where I can keep an eye on them while the moisture level is slowly reduced to about fifteen percent. Then we shell the kernels off the cob the old-fashioned way with a corn-sheller that rubs the ears together. Ordinary shelling equipment has rough metal burrs that would bruise the kernels and you know how I feel about that. So we make sure our shellers have the rough edges removed before we start shelling.
>
> Now we slowly condition the corn, drying it just enough so the moisture level in each kernel is at the exact point where it will pop its maximum. All of this may seem very exacting, but as some have said, "Trifles make perfection but perfection is no trifle."

We're also particularly fussy about sorting and cleaning our corn. First we sift out all our kernels that are a little too big or a little too small. Then a gravity separator rejects any kernels that are too dry and light, and any bits of cob that sneaked past. The acceptable kernels go into the polisher which rubs away any dust along with the little "bees wings" that attached the kernels to the cob. A stream of clean air leaves the shining, polished kernels ready to package.

[There] would be no use my taking these troubles to make you perfect corn if the package was not going to keep it in perfect condition until you use it. So I rejected the idea of bags or boxes. They let the moisture escape. And once you open a tin can, the rest of the corn could dry out and be less poppable than the first batch. That is why my Gourmet popping corn is sold only in jars with air-tight, screw-on lids. We put it up in two sizes, fifteen ounces and thirty ounces. If you put the lid on tightly after each use, the last batch in the jar will pop up as well as the first.

To make absolutely certain nothing has gone awry, we check random samples of the corn many times each day as it is packed. I want to be positive that. . .every kernel you get will be in prime popping condition—that it will pop up big, crisp, and tasty.

That is what you get when you buy a jar of Gourmet popping corn with my name on it.

Ah, yes: Orville's name on the jar. How Orville Redenbacher came to find his name used for his popcorn was one of his most celebrated stories, a story he relished telling to one and all.

You see, Orville and Charlie worked for four long years trying to sell popcorn producers on the excitement of their new popcorn. Orville traveled the country in his quest, talking to Jolly Time, National Oats, Pop Weaver, Cracker Jack, and all the other big companies—companies that were already customers of his other hybrid popcorn seed. The processors unanimously rejected Orville's popcorn and his radical concept that people would flock to pay more for premium popcorn.

Thoroughly frustrated, Orville and Charlie decided in 1970 to end the production of hybrid popcorn seed for the industry and come out with their own brand to prove all the processors wrong. They marketed it under the RedBow label and Orville got in his truck and personally visited store after store and shop after shop, trying to convince owners and managers to stock his popcorn.

Still, the stores and shops remained stubbornly disinterested, convinced a market was not waiting for the arrival of premium popcorn. In fact, the entire concept of gourmet food brands that were promoted as adhering to such higher standards than their competitors that they demanded a higher price and were well worth the additional cost—simply did not exist until Orville invented it. And not only did Orville invent the concept of gourmet foods, but he led the way with a product—his popcorn—that was not the obvious first choice for adopting the gourmet label.

But that was in the future. At the beginning and for years thereafter, just about the only customers RedBow had were the few popcorn devotees who drove down U.S. 30 to the Chester, Inc. plant to buy a five-pound sack.

The frustration continued to build and eventually Charlie turned to his friend and partner and asked Orville to journey into Chicago and hire someone to help develop a brand name and a package.

And so Orville jumped into his pickup truck and headed west to Chicago. He met with Gerson, Howe & Johnson, a well-known Chicago marketing and advertising firm based in the Wrigley Building. And what transpired there provided the grist for a tale Orville enjoyed repeating over the years to any reporter who asked how his popcorn got its name. In one television interview Orville answered the question this way:

"That's an interesting question, Candy," replied Orville. "I didn't know too much about marketing, so my partner, Charlie Bowman, said, 'Go into Chicago and hire a firm to help us develop a trade name.' They didn't know too much about popcorn. I didn't know too much about marketing. So I went back a week later to get their ideas, and see what kind of a brand name they had, and what kind of package they had, and they came up with the name Orville Redenbacher—which was the same identical name my mother thought up eighty-three years ago. And then they charged me thirteen thousand dollars for the idea."

Of course, giving credit where credit is due, Gerson, Howe & Johnson did marry "Orville Redenbacher's" to "Gourmet popping corn," thus creating the union and name brand—Orville Redenbacher's Gourmet popping corn.

And so the popcorn had a great name and Orville had a terrific story.

Orville wasn't the first "real" person to represent his company. Proprietors had long hung their names in front of their stores as a seal of their concern and personal guarantee. From small stores grew big stores—witness R. H. Macy's and Sears Roebuck and Company.

Paul Revere created the first American brand name. The Revolution hero was also a renowned silversmith, and any surviving bowl or dish or candlestick of Revere Silver is a most valuable item indeed.

Another person whose name represented a famous product was Sara Lee, the teenage daughter of Consolidated Foods founder Charles Lubin. He named a new line of pies after her, and eventually the entire company, too. Through all these years, Sara Lee Lubin, now in her fifties, has never been in any commercials or ads, and continues to enjoy her anonymity.

They are all nice stories, even mildly amusing, just like Orville's.

So Chester, Inc. had a product, and now the product had a name. Now Orville Redenbacher's Gourmet popping corn needed some publicity.

Orville arranged for a demonstration of his popcorn at Marshall Field's in Chicago, one of the great department stores in the land. Orville placed his popper on a table, popped up some kernels and distributed them to the media and the public. The event attracted a young correspondent, Frank Mathie, from the local ABC affiliate (WLS-TV) in town, who became the first television reporter to interview Orville Redenbacher. Mathie distinctly remembers the day:

"A PR guy from Marshall Field's called and said, 'We've got this guy who makes Gourmet popcorn.' When I heard the name, I thought the company had made it up."

Mathie and his crew went anyway, and the reporter was pleasantly surprised. "I remember him as sort of charming in a country, Midwest way," said Mathie. "He was very relaxed, with the press and the public. And the popcorn was very good."

Still, Mathie had his doubts as to the future of the product. "I have to admit I wondered, 'Would people pay more for Gourmet popcorn?' "

Frank Mathie was right to ask that question because even though the day was a success, the issue remained unresolved for several years.

Nonetheless, the event set the tone for the marketing strategy, and also set the manner in which the promotions were conducted. In short order, Orville did everything. He organized the public relations, headlined at the public appearances, sold the popcorn to stores, drove the truck and made most of the deliveries. In fact, he even spent hours on the packaging line, screwing on lids and gluing on labels.

The first customers included Marshall Fields', the Churchill stores in Toledo, Byerly's in Minneapolis, and assorted midwestern gourmet grocery shops and supermarkets.

Slowly, Orville Redenbacher's Gourmet popping corn began to build a following in the Midwest, consistently attracting new customers and "consumers." Nonetheless, the product, one of eighty-two brands on the store shelves—and the most expensive—had a long way to go. Distribution was widely dispersed and uncertain, and many people—literally hundreds—wrote to Valparaiso in search of Orville's own:

> I am writing to you in desperation. We have used the last of your Gourmet popping corn and the Kroger store where I shop no longer has it in stock. I have searched everywhere for it, to no avail. Perhaps you can tell me where in the area it can be purchased. It truly is the best of popcorn....

∾

> ...I am unable to locate more. I was so happy to find a popping corn of good quality and, even though expensive, it is well worth it. Is there a way I can purchase this corn?

∾

(One letter, in particular, cheered Orville. It was from his old Purdue professor, Arthur Brunson:)

> When we returned last week from Florida we found a winter flood of mail, including your Christmas present of Gourmet popping corn. We appreciate the gift and especially the memories of the old friendship it brings back.
>
> Frequently, I get so disgusted with the popcorn breeders when they think that pounds per acre is the prime criterion. Of course, they check expansion carefully, too, but they forget that tenderness, flavor, and absence of hard hulls are so extremely important to the eater. The Orville Redenbacher popcorn is the answer for the critical consumer who wants the best...

Brunson's letter meant a lot to Orville, who was not only confounded but also angered by the refusal of both the processors and the public to recognize the virtue of his popcorn. Orville—sixty-four years old and the prosperous owner of a sizable company—found himself working harder than ever, with less to show for it. In the early spring of 1971, the pressure and the work sent Orville to the Valparaiso hospital with ulcers. To make this time truly horrific, Orville's beloved Corinne died of an incurable bleeding ulcer in the same hospital, while Orville was incapacitated with his illness.

In the midst of these professional problems and his personal tragedy, a small New Orleans food sales and distribution firm, Blue Plate Foods, Inc., discovered Orville Redenbacher's Gourmet popping corn and began test-marketing it in the Dallas-Fort Worth area. Blue Plate Foods was a subsidiary of giant Hunt-Wesson Foods, Inc., headquartered in Fullerton, California.

Blue Plate Foods selected three hundred households and had them compare Orville's popcorn and Jolly Time Popcorn. Orville's was the people's preference by an overwhelming percentage, and Blue Plate Foods was ready. Its parent company, Hunt-Wesson, conducted its own marketing tests with Orville's popcorn and became convinced the product had terrific national potential.

Orville was also ready to make a deal. He and Charlie agreed to license Blue Plate Foods to sell their popping corn, under the Orville Redenbacher's Gourmet label.

"I was ill and needed help," explained Orville in later years. "I had none of the marketing, advertising, or sales training—or even the financial resources to expand the sales except at my very slow, one-man pace."

Hunt-Wesson had Blue Plate market and sell the popcorn through Hunt-Wesson's marketing department and national sales force. Chester, Inc. committed to raising between seven thousand and ten thousand acres of popcorn, contracting with farmers throughout Indiana and Illinois.

Orville agreed to promote his popcorn, pledging to spend six months traveling the U.S. on a publicity tour. The tour was planned and executed by the Chicago-based firm of Daniel J. Edelman Public Relations Worldwide, and took on an intensity that was fierce and tenacious.

Orville's schedule, commencing in September 1972, was unrelenting: all day, six days a week, almost every week, for six months.

By this time, Orville had married Nina Reder, an old family friend and widow, and the two of them now set out across America.

Surviving typewritten schedules from the Edelman office tell the tale. The following excerpts are typical:

DENVER, COLORADO
Tuesday, November 7
9:30 A.M.: KOA Radio (ABC). 5-minute interview oriented toward agriculture.

10:30 A.M.: KMGH-TV (CBS). Interview by Bob Palmer. Popper and corn requested for use on air.

1:15 P.M.: WGN-TV (Ind). 8-10-minute live interview. Popper and corn requested.

2:00 P.M.: 7-minute taped interview with Merrie Lynn of *Today in Colorado*. Popper and corn requested.

3:30 P.M.: KIMM Radio (Ind). Taped interview. Popcorn recipes requested.

Wednesday, November 8
9:00 A.M.: Interview with business writer, *Denver Post*.

10:00 A.M.: Interview with *Rocky Mountain News* (circ: 205,415).

2:00 P.M.: KBTR Radio (Ind). Interview for 15 minutes.

(The day ended so Orville could catch a plane for Arizona, where the schedule began again the next morning.)

PHOENIX, ARIZONA
Thursday, November 9
8:00 A.M.: KOOL-TV (CBS). Live interview on *The Phoenix Show*.
9:30 A.M.: KOY Radio (Ind). 15-minute interview on *Valley Visitor Show*.
10:30 A.M.: Exclusive interview with food editor, *Phoenix Gazette* (circ: 102,276)
1:00 P.M.: KPHO-TV (Ind). Popper, corn and recipes requested for live show.
Friday, November 10
9:00 A.M.: KOOL Radio (CBS). 12-minute interview on *Inside Story*
10:00 A.M.: KMCR-FM (Education). 30-minute taping.
1:00 P.M.: KASA Radio (Ind). 10-15 minute interview.
3:00 P.M.: KHFP Radio (Ind). Live 5-10 minute interview.

While those were certainly busy schedules, it is important to note that both Denver and Phoenix were smaller cities back in the seventies. Orville's calendar was that much more hectic when the tour hit larger cities, not to mention the megacities such as Chicago, Los Angeles, and New York.

In truth, the schedule was more than hectic, more than unrelenting—it was downright grueling. A tour of this magnitude was more than a matter of simply showing up somewhere and spinning some amusing tales about popcorn. Edelman required a small army to implement the details of the expedition, from setting up the interviews, to coordinating the travel, to overseeing unexpected problems, to delegating a person in each city to meet Orville at the airport and escort him around town, to organizing parties and special events, to collecting copies of the articles and cassettes of the television and radio appearances afterward, to following up with thank-you letters to all kinds of people, on and on.

And at the heart of it all were Orville and Nina barnstorming around the land. They hit thirty-seven cities, racked up several hundred interviews, and reached literally millions of Americans. Orville didn't appear only on the usual morning news and afternoon talk shows, he showed up apparently everywhere. One somewhat unusual appearance was on the veritable and immensely popular *What's My Line?*, where "challengers" showed up before a celebrity panel that attempted to ascertain who the challenger was and what he did for a living or a hobby by asking questions that required yes-or-no answers.

It was a clever stroke, appreciating that Orville, in the middle of his tour, though becoming more familiar to the public, had not yet reached the saturation point where everyone automatically knew this new business hero and public phenomenon.

On February 28, 1973, host Larry Blyden invited "our next challenger" to enter and sign in.

Orville walked onto the stage to the studio audience's applause and signed his name on the blackboard.

"Where are you from, sir?" Larry asked.

"I'm from Valparaiso, Indiana," Orville said.

"I didn't know there was one," Larry replied. "That shows what I know. Valparaiso. Okay. Orville Redenbacher, panel, raises a product. We will now show the audience what product he raises."

The word "Popcorn" appeared on the television screen so the audience was in on the secret, and they responded with more applause.

"And let's start the questioning with Leonard Harris," Larry said.

"I assume from the use of the word 'raise' that it's something that grows," theater critic Leonard said. "It has a life."

"Yes," Orville said.

"That leaves it now for me to decide whether it be animal or vegetable. And may I take a guess at animal?"

"No," Orville said.

Arlene Francis, Broadway actress, was next. "May I take a guess that it's a vegetable?"

"Yes," Orville said.

"Is it something that you raise out of doors?"

"Yes," Orville said.

"Is it...does it ever grow to quite large heights?" asked Arlene.

"Well," interjected host Larry, "how high is a large height?"

"How high is up?" shot back Arlene.

"Yeah," said Larry.

"Well," Arlene decided, "high as an elephant's eye."

"Like a sunflower," Larry said. "That high?"

"Yes," Arlene said, finally, mercifully settling on her question.

"Does it grow that high?" Larry turned to Orville and inquired.

"No," Orville said.

Comedian Soupy Sales was on the line. "Is it grown underground?"

"No."

"Then may we assume it is not in the root family like carrots and turnips and things like that?" asked effervescent actress Anita Gillette.

"Yes."

"Does it grow up and have...does it have pods?" queried Anita.

"No."

The questions kept coming fast and furious.

"Is it something you don't use ordinarily as food?"

"Is it an accessory to the meal as a rule?"

"Is it anything in the fruit family?"

The panel was shrewdly honing in on the secret. Anita verbally pondered this and that, and got around to the point.

"It's something that you would sit around and eat while you're looking at television," she mused. "Is it something that...sort of like a...like a popcorn kind of thing?"

"It is exactly like popcorn!" exclaimed host Larry as the studio audience vigorously applauded as Orville sat and beamed.

Larry more formally introduced the challenger to the panel and the crowd. "Orville Redenbacher is the originator of Orville Redenbacher's Gourmet popping corn, distributed by Blue Plate Foods, Inc. Now, your popcorn, apparently, is a very special one. Why is that?"

"Well," Orville said, "we have been breeding popcorn seed for thirty-five years and this is a single cross hybrid that we produce so it has a popping expansion of forty-four-to-one, and we practically eliminate all of the hulls and guarantee a one hundred percent pop."

He said this rapidly and without a break or even a pause. It was as if he had been silent too long, too many dull yes and no replies, and now had seized upon this chance to get out some vital popcorn information in a rush.

"So if you're sitting there in the movie eating this, you're not going to get all that in your teeth," said Larry, honing in on the practical. "Is that the notion?"

"Right."

"How were you able to do that?" inquired Larry. This was right up Orville's alley.

"Well, we have a nursery at Valparaiso in the summertime, and one in Florida in the wintertime, and we've been breeding the corn each year, two generations a year, trying to develop a better hybrid."

"Is there a secret to it?"

Boy, was there ever. "Well, yes, it's part of..." Orville paused, apparently deciding not even a nationally syndicated show was worth giving away trade secrets. Changing gears, he headed down another path. "...and also, the other thing is to process it correctly and get every kernel with the exact amount of moisture—thirteen and a quarter percent so it will pop."

"Does it cost more than others do?"

"Yes, it does." This was never a fact Orville sought to hide. Rather, it was one of his selling points, a sort of tangible proof that his popcorn cost more because it was overtly better and worth it. In fact, on some company stationery, it actually said, "World's Most Expensive Popping Corn," with a trademark symbol beside the phrase. That's right—Orville made sure the five words were forever his own.

"Is it better?"

"Oh, yes," Orville said. "It's better…much better."

Arlene Francis interrupted this semi-scientific sideshow. "Are we going to get some?"

"Are we going to get some?" chimed in host Larry.

"I hope so," Orville said. "Yes."

And so they did.

Just another day at the new job for Orville.

Blue Plate Foods was ecstatic with Orville's performance. Jim Myers, a Hunt-Wesson vice president, said Orville was "a natural. I don't think we could find a man more likable or memorable than Orville." C. James McCarthy III, president of Blue Plate, said Orville "was a great person who devoted his life to one thing—making the best popcorn in the world."

AdWeek described Orville as "a wry caricature sprung from 'American Gothic,' an owlish codger with the deportment of a life-long prom chaperone…"

Orville traveled many miles, popped a great deal of popcorn, signed an endless number of autographs, and talked…and talked…and talked. And when he was finished, he had accomplished his goal. Orville Redenbacher's Gourmet popping corn had begun to gain public acceptance. Orville Redenbacher's Gourmet popping corn was well on its way to being a hit.

But still, it was only a beginning.

Lesson: Statistics, Just for Fun

We've discussed many of the ins-and-outs, the ups-and-downs, the whys-and-wherefores of popcorn. The tales, the history, the lore, the science—what does it all mean?

Some people would say that it all comes down to statistics. Some people would say that if it can't be measured and calculated, then it doesn't really count. Some people would say that if it can't be added together, then it doesn't add up.

I don't happen to be one of those people. But hey, maybe you are. Maybe you love statistics. Maybe you're just waiting for somebody to take all these pages, all these words, all this stuff, and transform them into something...numerical. This is your lucky day.

(A note before we commence: Much of the information in this chapter is gleaned from information published by the Popcorn Institute. The Popcorn Institute, which Orville helped found and is currently headed by Orville's old friend, Bill Smith, is fond of compiling facts and figures, which makes sense considering that it's a trade association representing the popcorn processors and the popcorn industry. Nonetheless, believe it or not, other organizations, including The Consumers' Union and The United Fruits and

Vegetable Association, also gather popcorn information, assuredly for their own special purposes.)

Popcorn has become increasingly popular, as proved by the steadily rising sales. In 1970, 353 million pounds of unpopped popcorn were sold. Ten years later, in 1980, that amount had risen to 568 million pounds of popcorn. Ten years after that, in 1990, the figure had jumped to 938 million pounds of popcorn. A year later, popcorn sales had passed the one billion pound mark, and they keep going up.

Americans devour more than 17 billion quarts of popcorn annually. That's *17 billion quarts*, which breaks down to sixty-eight quarts for every man, woman, and child in this great and ravenous country. Seventy percent of that popcorn is consumed at home, while the rest is eaten in movie theaters, sports stadiums, and other places.

Americans produce the vast majority of the world's popcorn, and also consume most of it.

Los Angeles is the world champ when talking about popcorn consumption, with New York ranking a close second. Baltimore, Washington D.C., Milwaukee, Chicago, and Boston follow in the next five spots.

And popcorn isn't only for people—veterinarians put popcorn on their short list of human foods approved for dogs, which also includes peanut butter and raw nuts.

Yet for all this munching and crunching, you'd have to eat fully one hundred forty-eight cups of plain popcorn to gain a miserable, single pound.

If you should happen to prefer your popcorn in massive quantities, one hundred thirty-two cups of the stuff provides as much calcium as one eight-ounce glass of milk.

So where exactly does all this popcorn come from?

Almost all of the nation's popcorn is grown in the great Midwestern corn belt. By far, Indiana plants and harvests more than

any other state, as only befits the home state of Orville
Redenbacher. In 1994, Indiana planted and harvested over seventy-
seven thousand acres of popcorn. (The number of acres harvested
is sometimes a bit less than the number of acres planted, given the
vagaries of the weather. However, the hardiness of the popcorn and
the skill of the American farmer have rendered these amounts
almost always the same in every state, every year.) Illinois was number two, planting and harvesting over thirty-five thousand acres of
popcorn. Occupying the third spot was Nebraska, at almost twen-
ty-two thousand acres. Right behind was Ohio, nudging up to fifteen thousand acres. At eight thousand acres was Kansas, followed
by Iowa at more than seven and a half thousand acres. Dropping
down to over four thousand acres was Missouri, and then Kentucky
with just under four thousand acres. Michigan was next with not
quite two thousand acres. Six other states—Colorado, Minnesota,
Oklahoma, Pennsylvania, Texas, and Wisconsin—together with the
Canadian province of Ontario, pushed up the total yield another
eight and a half thousand acres.

The aggregate acreage for all of North America for 1994 was 183.9
thousand acres planted and 182.3 thousand acres harvested.

Every year brings a different set of farming realities, a different set
of natural factors, a different set of problems and priorities. For
example: 1995 did not prove as fertile a year for the popcorn farming community, and the yield was lower.

In 1995, Indiana planted and harvested just over sixty-three thousand acres of popcorn. The total for Illinois for that same year was over
seventeen thousand acres planted, and over seventeen thousand acres
harvested. Ohio took over third place from Nebraska in 1995, con-
tributing almost eleven thousand acres to the national gross. Nebraska
chipped in almost nine thousand acres of its own.

Adding smaller but still significant amounts of popcorn to the
aggregate is Kansas at more than five thousand acres, Kentucky at

just under five thousand acres, Iowa at almost three and a half thousand acres, and Michigan at not quite five hundred acres. The six other states and the Canadian province previously mentioned pitched in another five and a half thousand acres.

So for those keeping score at home, the entire sum equals one hundred twenty-thousand acres of popcorn planted and harvested, more or less.

Many other statistics remain to be uncovered: the percentage of yellow popcorn versus white popcorn, yield per acre per state, market purchases, the fact that popcorn is the only food that expands forty times in size when cooked, and so on.

Nonetheless, though it will assuredly prove a disappointment to many, it might be time to put an end to all this merriment and return to the main thrust of this tale, to Orville and his long and honorable journey.

The irony, of course, is that the man himself would have relished this roll of facts and figures. Orville spent days, weeks, months, literally years collecting and studying, measuring and weighing, calculating and computing all the numbers, data, material, and values—all the tangible manifestation of his ideas, hopes, and work—all the statistics—in his quest for the perfect popcorn.

And it worked. It certainly, absolutely worked. He took his research and experiments and statistics, and he applied them to his goal, his dream, and he accomplished exactly what he set out to do. How many of us can claim that? How many of us end up exactly where we set out to go at the start of our journey? A famous writer once said, "Life is the slow wearing away of hope and confidence," a depressing thought if there ever was one, but that unhappy fate was simply not acceptable to Orville. Think about it: Poor boy grows up to achieve fame and fortune doing exactly what he wants to do. What is the statistical probability of that? Rare, indeed.

14

The Pop Only Gets Louder and Larger

In 1974, Hunt-Wesson decided to sell off Blue Plate Foods. Regardless, the conglomerate was so enthused about the response to Orville's popcorn that it removed the agreement with Chester, Inc. from Blue Plate's portfolio and retained it for Hunt-Wesson.

One year later, it was Orville and Charlie's turn to reach an important decision. They resolved "to sell the whole works"—the popcorn business, in other words. The partners went to the Hunt-Wesson hierarchy and asked if the corporation was interested in a deal.

Hunt-Wesson most certainly was.

Negotiations began that fall and were concluded almost a year later. On July 1, 1976, the Orville Redenbacher's Gourmet popping corn business operations and property were sold from Chester, Inc. to Hunt-Wesson, the two parties agreeing that Hunt-Wesson would use the name of Orville Redenbacher's Gourmet popping corn in perpetuity.

By this time, and in just five years, Orville's popcorn had gone from virtual nonexistence to garnering the largest share of the U.S. popcorn consumer market. This was so even though the retail

price of Orville's Gourmet popping corn was about twice that of
the competition.

Both Orville and Charlie recognized that they might have sold out
too soon, that the business was just starting to take off. But several
factors had influenced their decision. On one hand, the men were
interested in pursuing other business interests with Chester, Inc. On
another, neither had children who were interested in following their
fathers into the popcorn business. And finally, perhaps the most crucial issue was one of timing. As Orville said, "I'm sure if my partner
and I had been fifteen years younger, we would never have sold it. We
knew we could get to the place they [Hunt-Wesson] were, but it
would have taken us fifteen years to do what they did in five."

And so Orville and Charlie pocketed their profits and moved on.
Except, for Orville, moving on meant staying pretty much right where
he was. He had signed a second, separate contract, in which he agreed
to work for the rest of his life as the persona and promoter of what
was still, at least emotionally and philosophically, Orville's popcorn.

Orville was crucial, it was as simple as that. The powers-that-be
at Hunt-Wesson recognized that a large part of the reason behind
the success of Orville Redenbacher's Gourmet popping corn was
Orville Redenbacher. He was a natural salesman, unaffected and
appealing. He sold without looking like he was trying to sell anyone
anything. He had the gift.

Straight promotion engagements and publicity appearances
remained on Orville's agenda, but now television commercials were
thrown into the mix. Botsford Ketchum, a leading San Francisco
advertising agency, created the spots.

In 1976, Orville starred in the first of many national television
commercials. His simple, direct style was all his own, and was surely
different from the usual actor-driven spot, full of slick enthusiasm and
false promises. Orville sold popcorn, he sold it as straightforward as
imaginable, he stood on the set and popped it up and the proof was

right there in the bowl on the screen. It was a smart approach, playing to Orville's strengths—honesty and sincerity—and Ketchum
employed those strengths for all they were worth.

So there was Orville, in his very first television commercial, seated at a table, wearing a somewhat oversized bow tie, white and gray
hair parted in the middle, curling backwards and to the sides, large
black glasses set firmly on the bridge of his nose, looking directly
into the camera. His manner was easy and friendly, though neither
frivolous nor irritating. Orville's script went like this:

"Hello. I'm Orville Redenbacher from Valparaiso, Indiana. And this
is four ounces of my Orville Redenbacher's Gourmet popping corn."

Orville pours the unpopped kernels into a popper before him.

"And this is four ounces of your ordinary popping corn."

He pours these kernels into a second popper. The scene cuts,
allowing for a time lapse, and Orville is watching both poppers
shake and crackle and pop their popcorn. Orville looks at the popper burdened with the ordinary popcorn.

"That's popping okay," allows Orville, but then he turns his gaze
upon his popper, and his voice quickly rises in excitement.

"But look at mine, it's blowing the top right off of the popper!"

And, in fact, it really is, the top of the popper is bouncing off
under the pressure of all those superior kernels.

"My Gourmet popping corn pops up lighter and fluffier than
ordinary corn." Orville reaches in, grabs a handful and munches.
He gives the unseen audience a little reassuring nod.

"Eats better, too," he says, and pours his triumphant popcorn
into a bowl. "See any old maids?" he asks, without explaining to
any innocents out there what the term means. "Near one hundred
percent pop."

Just enough time for the big finish.

"Orville Redenbacher's Gourmet popping corn. Try it."

The camera closes in on the jar, and Orville's hand gives the lid
an affectionate pat.

TV history was made.

Orville's fame never bothered Charlie Bowman. After all, even though
he benefited from his partner's work, many in Charlie's position would
have demanded their moment in the sun. But Charlie didn't care.

"Orville was a brass buttons and blue ribbons man," Charlie said,
on more than one occasion. "He loved the spotlight and the public
attention. I'm just the opposite. I don't."

For his part, Orville was continually surprised by his public
renown and his entertainment work. As he told a reporter, "It's
something I never dreamed of doing."

Nevertheless, Orville adapted very quickly and smoothly, enjoy-
ing the ride. And that was a good thing, because that ride didn't
stop, but kept going faster and higher, and Orville rode it all the
way to the top.

GOURMET POPCORN MAKES MILLIONS

Hunt-Wesson had a sales force of more than four hundred to ensure
that Orville's popcorn was in every store. The efforts of the corporation's sales force, combined with Orville's labors, meant that Orville
Redenbacher's Gourmet popping corn grossed $30 million in 1978.

Simultaneously, Hunt-Wesson was also changing. Hunt-Wesson
Foods, which owned the Orville Redenbacher's Gourmet popping
corn division, had joined with Canada Dry Corporation and McCall
Corporation in 1968 to form Norton Simon, Inc. a billion-dollar
corporation. While Norton Simon was headquartered in New York,
Hunt-Wesson stayed in Fullerton, California. In 1979, Hunt-
Wesson sales passed the $1 billion mark.

In 1983, Norton Simon, Inc. was purchased by Esmark, Inc., a
Chicago-based food and consumer product conglomerate. One year

later, Esmark agreed to be sold to Beatrice Companies, Inc. Beatrice was taken private by the investment firm of Kohlberg, Kravis & Roberts, becoming BCI Holding Company. Finally, BCI was acquired by ConAgra, Inc., based in Omaha, Nebraska, the absolutely colossal food multinational.

Orville was impressed with the company his popcorn was keeping, noting that with each merger and every buyout, "We keep becoming a smaller percentage of the total."

BACK TO WORK

Orville and his grandson Gary are seated on a park bench. Gary is a younger version of Orville; there is no mistaking the family resemblance.

Gary was Gary Fish, son of Billie Ann Redenbacher and Keith Fish. Later on, as he became more involved with his grandfather and the business, he legally changed his name to Redenbacher. Remember, Orville had three daughters, so Gary necessarily had to have a different last name from his grandfather.

The idea of using a grandson in the commercial was proposed by Ketchum Advertising. Since Orville had eight grandsons, the agency conducted a series of interviews and tests before choosing Gary, who today is an attorney specializing in children's issues.

Orville made it clear that he had nothing to do with the selection process.

In any event, on that park bench sat two Redenbachers in bow ties. The birds are singing while the men glance through a book. The following words appear on the screen as the announcer solemnly intones them: "Orville and Gary Redenbacher on overachieving."

Orville speaks. "This picture was taken when I was a senior in high school, which was my last year in the 4-H club. These were some of the ribbons I accumulated over the years."

The audience sees a photo of a stunningly young Orville, actually wearing a suit and bow tie, and literally covered with ribbons awarded for all kinds of farm-related activities. That face, that figure, couldn't possibly be anyone other than Orville Redenbacher.

Now it's Gary's turn. "He's always overachieving in 4-H and in popcorn. He likes to show that his popcorn pops up lighter and fluffier."

A table is positioned before them and a popper is going crazy as the kernels inside dance, expand, and explode. The rising popcorn pushes the lid off the popper.

"There we go, Grandpa," says Gary. "Popping the top off once again."

"That's the way I like to see things go," says Orville. "I like to see it go to its very highest possibility."

"Then it blows the top off every time," adds Gary.

"That's right" Orville says.

"That is overachievement," states Gary. "But it gives up great popcorn every time."

Exactly so.

Cut and print.

Gary, just as the other Redenbacher grandchildren, came by his popcorn expertise honestly. As Orville once explained to a television reporter, "We could always use extra help and Gary would visit in the summertime, when I was working in the nursery and in the seed fields. In the seed fields, we plant two rows of males, then six rows of females, then two rows of males, then six rows of females, and so on. That's the way we cross them and make good hybrids. Gary was always asking questions, and one day he said, 'Grandpa, how do you tell the difference between the male kernels and the female kernels?' I said, 'Well, that's easy. You just turn them over and look.' "

PHILANTHROPIC ACTIVITIES

Orville and Nina bought a condominium in Coronado, California, across the bay from San Diego. Consciously grateful for the good life he enjoyed, Orville spent a great deal of time and effort devoted to philanthropic causes. In 1954, President Dwight Eisenhower had started the People-to-People Program, which sought to promote understanding between peoples and nations through individual contact and personal and professional exchange. On behalf of furthering those aims, Orville jumped in with both feet, eventually becoming one of the organization's directors. He journeyed to no less than one hundred thirty-four nations, often leading agricultural groups.

That wasn't his only charitable activity, of course. He remained active with the Kiwanis Club his entire life, serving the association for sixty-five years, establishing a record for continual, active membership. And he never neglected serving the national 4-H organization, recalling his own days as a young member back in Clay County.

Then there was the national Easter Seals program, to which he lent his name and contributed substantial funds; as well as his support for the Purdue Alumni Association and the Purdue University President's Council.

He and Gary sponsored the 1992 United States National volleyball teams. In 1989 they underwrote a scholarship program for adult students either returning to complete interrupted college careers or pursuing higher education for the first time. Called Orville Redenbacher's Second Start Scholarship Program, in 1995 it provided $1,000 grants to twenty-five older students chosen from fourteen thousand applicants. "It is designed," Orville explained, "to help adults with an entrepreneurial spirit make a second start in life with a college education."

In 1996, the funds for the Second Start Scholarship program were channeled into an endowed scholarship to be established at Orville's alma mater, Purdue University. This scholarship will perpetually honor Orville Redenbacher among students of agriculture, forever reminding them of his impact in their chosen field.

Naturally, popcorn was still king with Orville, and he still traveled across the country on behalf of his Gourmet popcorn. He was quite the polished albeit homespun speaker. Rather frequently, Orville would introduce a speech by saying, "My subject tonight is sex."

Orville would pause, watching the audience glance at one another in surprise, and then launch into his talk about the sex life of the popcorn plant and the breeding methods required to obtain hybrids.

"Well," he would say, "it was fun while it lasted."

COMMERCIAL TIME

Orville stands right before the camera, a jar of his popcorn in hand.

"Hello, I'm Orville Redenbacher." As if anyone wouldn't know.

The camera pulls back to show Orville standing beside "Madam Sasha," a fortune-teller, and two empty poppers waiting before them. Two cards with big question marks on them are propped up against the poppers.

Orville asks, "Does Madam Sasha know which popcorn is my famous Gourmet popping corn?"

Madam Sasha's reaction is as exaggerated as her voice is accented (as you would expect from a fortune-teller). "Madam Sasha knows all," she boasts.

Orville is not convinced. "Let's see…"

Orville pours two loads of unpopped kernels into the poppers, and off they go. As the popcorn starts popping, Madam Sasha confidently makes her selection.

"*That* is yours!" she proclaims.

But, alas, the good Madam is wrong, as Orville is forced to note. "No, this is mine."

That is obvious to anyone who knows anything, because, as Orville points out, one group of kernels is popping "so much bigger,'n' fluffier, it's blowing the top off the popper! And look—most every kernel pops."

Madam Sasha attempts to recover. "I knew that."

Orville addresses the camera as Madam Sasha munches away.

"Taste my Gourmet popping corn," he says, and gives his typically understated big finish. "You'll like it better or my name isn't…Orville Redenbacher."

HAPPY BIRTHDAY, ORVILLE

In 1987, Orville turned eighty-years old. The celebration turned into a national public relations triumph for both Orville and his popcorn. A huge birthday card comprised of four-by seven-foot panels covering eighteen hundred square feet was transported eight thousand miles around the country, through fourteen major American cities and countless smaller communities, aboard a special Orville Redenbacher birthday train. One hundred thousand men, women, and children signed the card.

The realm of celebrity didn't miss out on the commemoration. Cards arrived from Debbie Reynolds, Vanna White, Joan Rivers, Angie Dickinson, Mike Ditka, and Florence Henderson. And that was only a small sample:

> From Hollywood…
> From the first time I tasted your corn, I knew you were the man for me. I'm a big fan—you make me smile.
> Happy Birthday, Orville. Many more!
> —Whoopi Goldberg

To North Dakota...

You and I have a lot in common. We're both now in our eighties—although I've got you beat by a couple of years. And we've both been described as the "King Of Corn."

However, I have always been rather pleased with that title and I'm sure you are too.

Have a wonderful 80th birthday party, and every good wish for many more birthday parties to come.

> Very sincerely,
> —Lawrence Welk

There were those whose shtick knew no bounds...

It was Lot who said, when his wife was turned into a pillar of salt, "Salt I got. Popcorn I need!"

> —Red Buttons

Those whose enthusiasm was in the same category...

The N.C. State Wolfpack wish you a happy 80th birthday!!

You have brought great joy and happiness to several generations of popcorn lovers.

Happy birthday!!!

> Best wishes,
> —Jim Valvano

Those who tended to the formal...

Let me join with your many friends in Valparaiso in wishing you a very happy 80th birthday.

While some may enjoy discussing the research and the marketing, Marilyn, the children and I enjoy the popcorn!

May you have many more birthdays and continued success and happiness.

> Sincerely,
> —Dan Quayle

Those who took a casual approach...

Attaboy, Orville.

> —Gregory Peck

To the absolutely concise...

Happy B.D. Orville.

> —Clint Eastwood

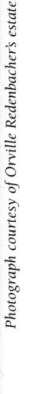

Orville with Henry and Hy Smith (in hat), two of the owners of Princeton Farms.

In 1940 Orville managed Princeton Farms' 12,000 acres—the largest farm in Indiana. This Angus auction was one of his many responsibilities.

The entrance to Chester, Inc.

Chester, Inc.'s popcorn receiving plant.

The rising demand for liquid fertilizer in the 1950s prompted Chester, Inc., to build this production plant for its new product, KV Liquid Fertilizer.

From 1952–1975 Orville maintained an office in Chester, Inc., where he researched and examined corn.

Cornstalks are tagged for development purposes.

Near Homestead, Florida, Orville shows how to pollinate hybrid popcorn seed.

Orville working on cornstalks in the nursery near Homestead, Florida.

In Brookston, Indiana, Orville examined corn as it was lifted by an elevator to a grain bin, where it was stored until it was shelled and shipped to Valparaiso to be processed and packaged.

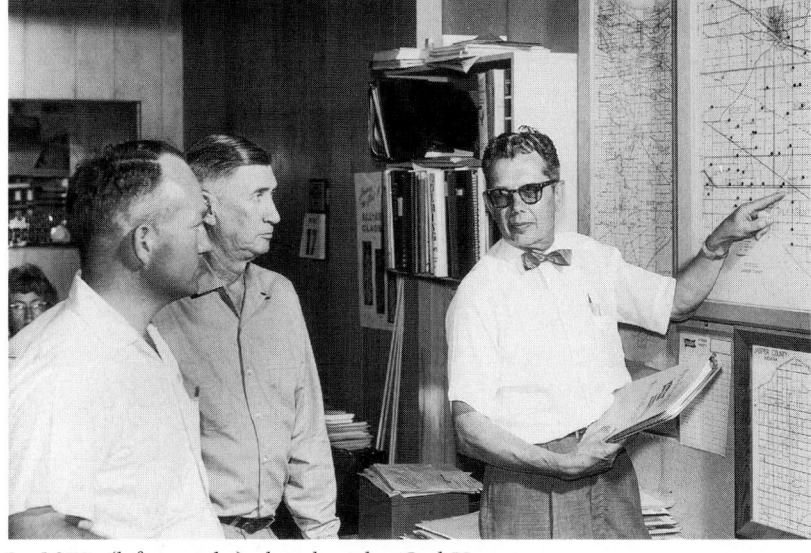

In 1955, (left to right) plant breeder Carl Hartman,
bookkeeper Harvey Evans, and Orville reviewed a plan for Chester, Inc.

Friends and partners, Orville and Charlie Bowman.

In 1974, Orville still tended his beloved field.

Orville measuring the "popping" volume of his popcorn.

At the popcorn "ball," Orville was serenaded by the famous Gaslight Club Girls in 1972 in Chicago.

The Hee-Haw cast surprised Orville with a cake decorated with popcorn made out of icing.

Orville showed the proper way to cook popcorn to Billye Williams on the *Today in Georgia* show.

Then Vice President Dan Quayle and his wife, Marilyn, take time out to visit a fellow Hoosier.

Orville with the Queen of the 1994 Valparaiso Popcorn Festival, the last time he attended the festival which has been honoring him for 17 years.

In 1983, four generations of Redenbachers (and one professional actor, Shep the dog) were featured in print and television advertisements. It was the first time Orville's grandson, Gary, appeared in any advertisements. The rest of the cast included: (top row, left to right) son-in-law Jim Tuminello, daughter Gail Tuminello, great-grandson J. Grant Gourley, granddaughter-in-law Martha Gourley, grandson J. Kent Gourley; (seated) Nina and Orville Redenbacher, daughter Carole Lister; (front row) grandson Gary Fish-Redenbacher.

Gary was chosen by Hunt-Wesson's advertising agency, Ketchum, to work with his grandfather and promote popcorn.

In 1994, Orville was Honorary Grand Marshall of the Peru Circus City Festival Parade in Peru, Indiana.

The successful duo of Orville and Gary spoofed the movie industry with advertisements including the accompanying three: "Orville of Arabia," "The Hunt for Redenbacher,"…and, of course, "Raiders of the Lost Kernel."

Orville and Charlie Bowman remained lifelong friends.

Orville Redenbacher's Gourmet popping corn hot-air balloon.

Eventually, Orville became a natural model and posed with ease for print advertisements.

To the absolutely classic…
Happy birthday, Orville! I send my love.
—Lucy

The media couldn't be denied during Orville's grand birthday tour of the United States, and he appeared on apparently every radio station, every television show, and in every newspaper that spewed forth its opinions and reports unto this nation's population.

On June 23, 1987, Orville appeared on *The Morning Show*— Regis Philbin and Kathie Lee Gifford's daily celebrity talk show. *The Morning Show* was one of the more important venues, as far as this business was concerned, as important in its own way as the Letterman program. Orville was Orville, and Regis and Kathie Lee stayed true to their roles, and that, of course, is what television is all about.

"Here he is," announced Regis, "the Grandpop of popcorn, and what a great story this is, too. Currently on a grand tour of the United States to celebrate his eightieth birthday and his Gourmet popcorn, here's Orville Redenbacher."

Orville rather briskly strode onto the set. A large, old-fashioned popcorn machine, the kind that's on wheels so the vendor can push the contraption along the street, was also on stage, filled with popcorn.

Orville greeted his hosts and sat down. Another small, electric popper was on a table before the trio.

"Orville," said Regis, "you look like you just stepped out of a Norman Rockwell painting."

"He sure does!" agreed Kathie Lee.

Regis had a point. Orville was wearing a seersucker suit and a red bow tie with the white popcorn kernels, apparently the same bow tie he wore on the David Letterman show.

Orville's attention, however, was fixed on that electric popper. He rose from his seat and removed a plastic cover from the top of the popper. Steam immediately poured from the popper and loud popping could be heard as the kernels burst open.

Satisfied, Orville sat back down and gave a very short lecture on proper popcorn popping technique.

"One of the most common mistakes is to leave the top on," said Orville. "You leave the top on and the steam will accumulate and drop back down and make the popcorn go soft."

"Well," Regis said, "that's our crew." He gave a disapproving glance to the side, going for the laugh. His effort was briefly rewarded.

Kathie Lee inquired about microwave popping, still a relatively new thing, and Orville replied that microwave popularity was steadily increasing, and currently had grabbed about half of the popcorn market. (Today, microwave popcorn overwhelms the competition, snagging about 90 percent of retail popcorn sales.)

Meanwhile, the electric popper was at the height of its excitement and causing quite a racket, drowning out the conversation—a fact that did not go unnoticed by Regis.

"Between that poofed skirt and this," Regis exclaimed, referring to Kathie Lee's attire and the popcorn, "I can't think anymore! Look at that sucker go!" Now Regis was only referring to the popper. "Boy, it's really filling up nicely."

"It's supposed to expand about forty-four-to-one," Orville said, keeping his eye on what was really important.

"Now Orville," continued Regis, "do you have the best popcorn in the world?" Talk about your softball questions.

"Oh, sure," said Orville.

The audience gave an appreciative laugh as Orville smiled. He was as natural as air on television, but he was also a pro, and knew the game well.

"Yeah," said Regis. "Now Orville, what makes your popcorn better than somebody else's?" Regis picked up a stalk of popcorn, an unblemished, yellow cob, and inspected it as the camera closed in for the audience at home to see. "I mean, after all, it all comes from the same corn, doesn't it?"

In response, Orville grabbed a jar of his popcorn and held it up. "It's got a better picture on the jar probably."

Regis, Kathie Lee, and the audience laughed.

"It's a different hybrid entirely," Orville said.

"You bred this corn, didn't you?" Kathie Lee said.

"Yes," Orville said.

"See," Kathie Lee said, "he knows his popcorn, Reeg."

Orville rose once more and pulled the plug on the popper. He then turned the popper over.

"I'm doing this to keep it from burning," Orville said.

Orville separated the popping device from the bowl holding the popped kernels, and there it was, a bowl filled with hot popcorn.

"Wow," commented Regis, "that's nice."

"And hardly any kernels aren't popped," added Kathie Lee. "That's my big problem. How do you get. . .you know, you have a few kernels left in the bottom."

"The kernels that are left are called old maids," said Orville.

"They're old maids," repeated Kathie Lee.

"They're old maids," Regis said. "What does that mean?"

The audience started chuckling.

"What?" Kathie Lee said. "What a sexist guy, huh?" Kathie Lee tossed a knowing frown at the audience.

As was his habit, Orville was on to the issue that interested him, leaving unanswered one of the great popcorn questions.

"The breeding makes the quality," said Orville. "This is a hybrid, this is the same corn that's in that jar"—Orville pointed to his jar— "which really makes the quality. But if you get the exact moisture in every kernel of corn, thirteen and a quarter percent, thirteen and a half percent, then every kernel should pop. A lot of times we'll make a bet and come out with one hundred percent corn."

Regis held up that cob. "Beautiful looking corn, isn't it?"

"Yeah," Kathie Lee said. "It doesn't even look real, it's so unusual."

"One of the most common questions we get," said Orville, "is how do you make popcorn out of corn. You really don't. Popcorn is a distinct variety. It's the oldest food item we have."

"It's thousands of years old," Kathie Lee said slowly, recalling those research notes compiled by the production staff.

"Five thousand six hundred," Regis said, clearly more familiar with the notes. "Right, Orville?"

"Five thousand six hundred years old," concurred Orville.

Regis wondered who started this corn popping binge, and Orville talked about the Incas, and the Bat Cave in New Mexico which predated the Incas, and then about how he got started, and finally wound around to how nutritious popcorn actually was.

While Orville was speaking, Regis and Kathie Lee began munching on the popcorn produced by the electric popper.

"Do you know what I do when I want to lose five pounds in a week?" inquired Kathie Lee. "And I know doctors are going to kill me…"

"When do you want to lose five pounds in a week?" asked a skeptical Regis.

"Right before a commercial or something like that," replied Kathie Lee, "when you're pretty desperate. I eat a nice lunch, very nutritious and all that, and at night, when I'm getting hungry, I do a big thing of popcorn, and I do that for a week, and it works."

"Yeah," Regis said, "but Orville, you need a little salt, don't you?" Regis makes a somewhat unpleasant face as he eats more popcorn.

"Yes, you do," Orville said, "you need regular popcorn salt."

"No," insisted Kathie Lee, still focused on her own diet routine, "I stay away from the butter and salt."

"It's not good for you," Regis said, "but it sure tastes good."

That provided another opening for Orville. "That's why we use the butter-flavored oil, so you don't have to add any butter and the calories."

Before long, it was time for the big round-up, and it was Kathie Lee's job to get it going.

"You've made popcorn your life," she began, "but we've heard that if you had a choice, you would always choose pie over popcorn. Is that true?"

"No" Orville said, "I think the choice is that I'd always eat pie first."

Uh-oh. Research foul-up, throwing the whole gag out of kilter. To make matters worse, Orville kept talking.

"Whenever you have pie at a meal, I eat pie first and then if I can eat anything else, I eat the rest of the meal. But popcorn is really my first choice."

Kathie Lee gallantly kept pressing on. "But you weigh one hundred thirty-two pounds, Orville."

Orville responded that popcorn is an excellent diet food, only compounding the rapidly unraveling ending. Regis already figured that this was heading south, and started to give a wry smile, overtly prepared to leave Kathie Lee out there by herself.

"Popcorn is your favorite food," he said in deadpan style. "There's no doubt about it."

Nothing could stop Kathie Lee. "Would you trade all of this popcorn here to your right…"

"No," Regis said, "he wouldn't."

"You're going…," sputtered Kathie Lee, finally faltering, "for one pie and give all the popcorn to the audience."

"You're a popcorn man!" concluded Regis, the audience in on the joke.

Orville graciously let Kathie Lee out of the trap. "I would do it to get rid of the popcorn, yes, but.…"

"No," persisted Regis, "he'd rather have popcorn."

"I'm going to kill you, Regis," warned Kathie Lee.

"I'm telling you right now," Regis said, "he'd rather have his popcorn."

Regardless, Kathie Lee brought out a coconut custard pie, Orville's favorite, and all that popcorn waiting inside that old-fashioned popper was distributed to the studio audience.

And that's show biz.

By the by, Orville's favorite snack—after popcorn—was the simple jelly bean, which he placed on trays and jars throughout his home.

Popcorn flavored, naturally.

And so the press and publicity dance spun round and round. One day *The Morning Show*, the next a satellite media tour.

The satellite tour is one of those strange innovations that provide local television anchors, correspondents, and talk show hosts the chance to do their thing quick and clean for two minutes of air time. The guest sits in a room and cameras are readied and makeup applied, and then the local stations line up and tune in, one by one, each allocated a certain time to delve deep albeit quickly into the topic at hand. One by one, over and over, the same questions, the same small talk, and then it's out and who's up at bat next? The point is to most efficiently employ the time of both the guest, who discharges a round of public relations responsibilities in one giant shot, and the stations, which are spared the expense and trouble of flying in the guest and reading his book or his clippings and researching him and what-not, all the while giving the audience the idea that the host and guest are closer, more familiar, than they actually are.

That's local TV.

And so Orville and Gary did their satellite bit, Houston, Minneapolis, Nashville, Indianapolis, Tampa, Orlando, and Dallas, all in a row, one after another, bang, bang, bang.

And did the media ask the same questions? The usual questions? Did they inquire as to why his popcorn was better? Did they ponder whether he really ate a lot of popcorn? Did they wonder if popcorn really was healthy for you? Did they ask if that bow tie was for real?

You know they did.

At the end of 1988, Orville showed up on *CBS This Morning*. Kathleen Sullivan was the host and she started with the bow tie.

"Now tell me about the bow tie," Kathleen said. "Is that all an image? A lot of people think that you're actually just a spokesperson."

"I didn't start wearing bow ties until I started high school," Orville replied, "and I've been wearing them ever since. No, I'm not a Betty Crocker."

And then they went on to talk about how Orville was always intrigued by the noble popcorn plant, and how when Purdue released the first hybrids its researchers produced in 1941, Orville had taken those hybrids and run with them, experimenting and working to perfect the plant. Kathleen asked a bunch of the expected questions, and then a few interesting ones as well.

"At sixty-three years old," Kathleen said, "you could have sold it off then. Why did you decide to really market it? You believed so strongly in this product that you stuck with it for forty years before it became nationally famous."

"Well," Orville began, "we made this breakthrough with this Gourmet variety in 1965 and we were the world's largest producers of hybrid seed at that time. We were supplying processors all over the United States and the world with popcorn seed. But I couldn't sell them on this marketing concept that people would like to have the opportunity to buy real, high-quality popcorn, and be willing to pay a premium for it."

Kathleen and Orville talked a bit more about popcorn and then Kathleen asked, "Do you feel you're as vital in your eighties as you were in your sixties?"

"I think I am," Orville said, "but when I get out, physically, I find I'm not. But I didn't want to retire completely, so this has worked out nicely."

"Mr. Redenbacher, what keeps you going? What keeps the spunk and the pop going?"

"I'd say the popcorn, but, uh..." Orville paused, considering. "There were two courses I had at Purdue that helped me out a lot. I played the sousaphone in the Purdue band, and that's where I learned to toot my own horn. I also ran track and cross-country, and I soon found out you don't win unless you stay out in front."

Orville used those two lines a lot, and they always got the laughs he expected. But that didn't mean they weren't true.

At Last—Recipes

In 1989, Hunt-Wesson published a small pamphlet entitled "Orville Redenbacher's Gourmet Guide to Popping Corn: A Special Collection of Redenbacher Family Recipes." On the cover's inside page, Orville had authored a letter to the reader:

> Hello, I'm Orville Redenbacher. As the father of three, grandfather of twelve, and great-grandfather of six, I know what it's like to satisfy a variety of family tastes....
>
> ...so my grandson Gary and I got together to create the Orville Redenbacher's Guide to Popping Corn just for you and your family. This booklet features plenty of popcorn recipes sure to satisfy everyone's taste buds, whether you crave spicy, sweet, light or festive foods.

Orville's appreciation for and enjoyment of his popcorn took on profound dimensions. No one who ever knew or even encountered Orville doubted that his devotion to his popping plant was based on his understanding of its unique properties.

Following are a handful of Orville's favorite recipes, presented for your satisfaction. We start simply, because at heart, that's who Orville was. His acknowledged preference was for unadorned popcorn—"a popcorn purist," he called himself—with merely a bit of salt on it.

Salt after popping, he counseled, and use fine-grained popcorn salt. It will cling more resolutely to the popcorn, and be far less likely to end up in the bottom of the bowl.

So simple. So perfect. So Orville.

FRUIT & THREE PUFF BREAKFAST CEREAL

We shall start with the lightest in calories, easiest on the waist, and progress into dark, forbidden territory from there.

Orville's sense of history never failed him. He not only knew his popcorn lore and his popcorn chronicles, he honored and relished them. The following recipe is called "Fruit & Three Puff Breakfast Cereal," and it recalls the early colonists' formula for this puffed breakfast treat. To achieve this historical and nutritious meal, follow these simple steps.

1 quart of popped Orville's best

1 packet of Equal® sweetener (The blue package is key, because saccharin-based substitutions may result in a somewhat bitter taste, and good old regular sugar blows away that minuscule eighty-nine calorie feat)

¼ teaspoon of cinnamon

A pinch of nutmeg

1 cup of puffed wheat

1 cup of rice-type cereal

½ cup of any two—shredded coconut, banana chips, raisins, chopped dates, chopped fruit roll-ups, or peanuts. (And only two, though don't ask me why as I hail from the school of the-more-the-merrier. But, of course, this is Orville's recipe, and he assuredly knows best.)

Place the popcorn in a large bowl. In a conveniently near small bowl, combine the Equal, cinnamon, and that pinch of nutmeg. Having accomplished that task, sprinkle the mixture over the popcorn, tossing—and quoting precisely—"gently to coat." Add the remaining ingredients again doing that "tossing gently" thing to thoroughly mingle and merge.

Store this concoction in an airtight container in a cool, dry spot.

To serve, place ⅔ cup of cereal in a bowl. Pour ½ cup of milk over the feast, and presto—eight servings with which to delight eight loved or at least very well-liked ones—and at only 89 calories, 0 milligrams of cholesterol, 4 grams of fat, and 36 milligrams of sodium.

WAIST WATCHIN' POPCORN SNACK

Orville called this the "Waist Watchin' Popcorn Snack." Not a catchy title, perhaps, but the sentiment is direct enough. So…

2 quarts of Orville's own already popped popcorn,
Add
2 cups of unsalted, dry roasted peanuts
2 cups of pretzel sticks
1½ cups bite-size bran cereal squares
3 tablespoons of reduced-calorie margarine
1 tablespoon of prepared brown mustard
2 teaspoons of salt-free herbs and spices

With the ingredients arrayed before us, we must now face a large bowl and a small saucepan. Into the bowl we combine hot popcorn—and we stress hot—nuts, pretzels, and bran squares. Melt the margarine in the saucepan and add the mustard. Pour this mixture over the bowl's contents, and then sprinkle in the herb and spices. Toss well. Spread this coated corn on a baking sheet and bake at 350 degrees F for three to five minutes.

Done. Finished. Complete. We've now cooked, or shall we say prepared, 2½ quarts of the stuff.

Serve immediately or store in an airtight container.

And now for what you've been waiting for: a one-ounce serving has 126 calories, 0 milligrams of cholesterol, 8 milligrams of fat, and 173 milligrams of sodium.

Not as pure and purely low calorie as popcorn alone, but nothing to complain about either.

Good job, Orville.

GARY'S POWER CRUNCH COOKIES

Another light favorite was called "Gary's Power Crunch Cookies," and so named because Orville said it was grandson Gary's personal favorite.

3 cups of popped popcorn—Orville's, in case anyone was wondering.
1½ cups quick-cooking rolled oats
¾ cup of all-purpose flour
½ cup of raisins
½ tablespoon each of baking soda and cinnamon
¼ teaspoon of salt
¾ cup of firmly packed light brown sugar
½ cup of margarine—softened
1 tablespoon of water
1 tablespoon of vanilla

Now that all the players are assembled, combine the first seven ingredients in a medium-sized bowl. Then, in a large bowl, cream brown sugar with margarine, then stir in water and vanilla. Gradually add flour mixture, stirring well after each addition. By now we're facing something substantial. Drop dough from spoon onto ungreased 15-by-10-inch baking sheet.

Bake at 375 degrees F for ten to twelve minutes, or until golden brown. Believe it or not, when we remove that baking sheet, we'll be staring at two dozen delicious cookies, all at the itsy-bitsy price of 107 calories, 0 milligrams of cholesterol, 4 grams of fat, and 85 milligrams of sodium. That's 107 calories per cookie, of course, not for the entire batch.

BERRY GOOD FROZEN YOGURT PIE

The last low-cal combination is a real topper, a dessert sensation, an explosion of taste, a major fantasy number Orville liked to call "Berry Good Frozen Yogurt Pie." It's complicated but simple at the same time, a real yin-and-yang food creation.

4 cups of Orville Redenbacher's Gourmet popping corn, popped and slightly crushed. (Yes, that's right—we take our popcorn and slightly crush it. That might sound like sacrilege, but what must be done, must be done. For the greater good, of course.)

½ **tablespoon of lemon-flavored beverage mix** made with NutraSweet® brand sweetener—Remember the admonition about the bitter taste of saccharin-based sweeteners? Heed or beware.

1 quart of berry-flavored frozen yogurt, slightly softened

2 cups of frozen nondairy whipped topping, thawed

lemon slices are optional

In a large bowl, combine hot popcorn with dry beverage mix and we stress hot and dry—place in bottom and on sides of 9-inch pie plate. Gently spoon softened frozen yogurt on this popcorn shell, smoothing out to even surface. Top with thawed, non-dairy whipped topping.

Freeze this masterpiece, uncovered, for three hours or overnight. Garnish with lemon slices or lemon-coated popcorn.

Eight generous servings will be our reward, with 189 calories per five-ounce slice, 5 milligrams of cholesterol, 7 grams of fat, and an even 100 milligrams of sodium.

Now that's cooking!

GIGANTIC TURTLE CANDIES

Enough of this "good for you" nonsense—it's time to get down to what we all crave, what we all want, what our bodies and souls demand. Chocolate. Chocolate chips. White chocolate. Cream. Ice cream. Sugar. Almonds. Pralines…We want it all. We want the works.

Let's start with some tempting treats Orville nicknamed "Gigantic Turtle Candies."

1 quart of popped Orville's Gourmet popcorn begins the festivities
1 14-ounce bag of light caramels (and do remove the wrappers)
2 tablespoons of butter
2 tablespoons of milk, and—and this is big, or at least sizable—48 to 54 pecan halves. (Why the sudden casual, cook's choice? Don't ask why, just choose and move along.)
1 12-ounce bag of semisweet chocolate chips
1 tablespoon of shortening

Okay. All right. So far, so good. Now, place the popcorn in a large bowl and set to the side.

In a medium saucepan, over a medium-low flame, join in holy matrimony caramels, butter, and milk. Stir until smooth.

Meanwhile, on a lightly greased, wax paper-covered baking sheet, arrange groups of three pecans in a cloverleaf pattern, or the nearest approximation you can devise, without excessive straining. When the caramel is smooth, pour the delectable semi-solid goop over the popcorn, tossing gently to coat.

Let stand for two minutes or until the mixture holds its shape when spooned onto those patiently waiting nuts. Using two spoons, place a mound of caramel-coated popcorn onto the center of each pecan cloverleaf.

But that's not all. In a small saucepan, melt the chocolate with the shortening, then lovingly spoon over each caramel mound.

Chill for four hours or overnight, and awaken to sixteen to eighteen turtles.

Gigantic turtle candies, no less.

Be prepared to pay the piper to the tune of 347 calories for each two-ounce turtle, not to mention 4 milligrams of cholesterol, 25 grams of fat, and 79 milligrams of sodium.

MOCHA ALMOND CRUNCH

It's time for "Mocha Almond Crunch."

2 quarts of Orville's popped popcorn
½ cup of toasted, slivered almonds
1 cup of sugar
¼ cup of light corn syrup
1 tablespoon of butter
1 tablespoon of water
¼ teaspoon of cream of tartar
¼ teaspoon of salt

But there's more, as befits a lush, rich treat, so don't forget:

½ teaspoon of baking soda
1½ tablespoons of instant coffee
½ cup of semisweet chocolate chips—melted

Now take a breath and rest, and then get up and go, because it's time to assemble and cook!

In a large bowl, add together the popcorn and toasted almonds.

In a medium saucepan, over medium heat, bring the sugar, the corn syrup, the water, the butter, the cream of tartar, and the salt to a boil. Boil rapidly to the soft crack stage—270 degrees F on a candy thermometer should do it. Remove from the heat. Stir in the baking soda quickly but thoroughly. Add the instant coffee, stirring until well blended.

Working quickly, and that's no joke, pour the mixture over the popcorn, tossing gently to coat. Evenly spread the coated corn (Haven't we heard some of these phrases before?) onto greased wax paper.

Cool for five minutes.

Using a fork, drizzle the melted chocolate over the popcorn mixture. Allow to cool for four hours. Break into chunks and store—you guessed it—in an airtight container.

Each one-ounce serving will penalize the eater 116 calories, 2 milligrams of cholesterol, 4 grams of fat, and 61 milligrams of sodium.

But sometimes we have to suffer for art.

PRALINES, POPCORN & CREAM

I scream, you scream, we all scream for "Pralines, Popcorn & Cream." Now stop screaming and prepare to cook.

1 quart of popped Orville's own starts us off

⅔ cup of firmly packed dark brown sugar

¼ cup of butter

½ gallon of softened vanilla ice cream (Now we're talking!)

2 tablespoons of coffee-flavored liqueur are optional, though which of us in our right minds would leave it out?

In a large saucepan, stir together the first three ingredients, until the brown sugar and the butter are melted. Spread the popcorn and the brown goo onto a foil-lined 15-by-10-inch baking sheet.

Bake at 400 degrees F for eight minutes, and then cool for another ten.

Meanwhile, in a medium bowl, commingle the softened ice cream with the coffee-flavored liqueur. (Which no longer seems so optional, does it? I mean, now that you know you can add this liqueur zest to the mix, won't you seriously miss it if you don't?)

Stir the cooled, candied popcorn into the ice cream. Freeze until ready to devour—uh, serve.

If no one's been nibbling, we'll have a half gallon of the stuff.

This treat contains 69 calories for every ounce, 13 milligrams of cholesterol, 3 grams of fat, and 35 milligrams of sodium.

Now go ahead and scream.

PEANUT BUTTER & JELLY THUMBPRINT NO-BAKE COOKIES

Here's one that doesn't actually require cooking, assuming cooking demands an oven that is either baking or broiling or burning. Rather, let's put this under the "preparing" category.

So let's crowd around the kitchen and prepare... drumroll..."Peanut Butter & Jelly Thumbprint No-Bake Cookies."

2 quarts of Orville's popped popcorn
1 cup of light corn syrup
1 cup of Peter Pan® Creamy Peanut Butter
3 tablespoons of a favorite fruit jam. Strawberry, apricot, rasp-berry—not a displeasing fruit in the bunch.

Put the popcorn in a large bowl.

In a medium saucepan, over medium-high heat, bring the corn syrup to a boil, and boil for three minutes.

Stir in the peanut butter.

Now, get ready because it's time to work quickly. And working quickly, pour the peanut butter mixture over the popcorn, toss-

ing gently to coat. Allow to cool for ten minutes. Roll the popcorn mixture into eighteen two-inch balls. Press a thumb firmly
into the center of each ball. Fill each cookie center with half a teaspoon of jam.

Store those eighteen cookies in an airtight container.

Substitute chocolate kisses for jam in the center of each cookie if you like, or almost anything else that suits your fancy. The
choices are limited only by your imagination.

Going the traditional route yields a payload of 156 calories per
cookie, with 0 milligrams of cholesterol, 8 grams of fat, and 104
milligrams of sodium.

16

Orville to the End

As he demonstrated on his eighty-fifth birthday appearance on David Letterman's show, Orville was in remarkable physical and intellectual shape, walking with a firm step, answering with a fast quip. Genealogy certainly helped him maintain his health (hereditary luck of the draw), but so must have his unabated enthusiasm for his life and his work played a significant role.

Quite simply, there was something about popcorn that never lost any of its appeal to Orville. Around this time, he tried to explain to a reporter what it was that made popcorn so popular. Never mind the nutritional value and low cost and all the rest, he was talking about the core of the issue, at the most basic, unadorned level:

"I had a product that was a fun item," Orville said. "I had a product that was liked by people who were eighty-years old, as well as four years old, and was liked by people who lived from one coast to the other coast, from the Mexican border to the Canadian border. Everyone seems to like popcorn, because it is such a fun item."

Fun. That was something Orville never neglected or devalued. Fun was important, fun was meaningful. Fun was a feeling and a reality he brought to his family, and shared with his family, from swimming in the backyard pool in summer to gathering beside the tree at Christmas. And fun—that open, uncomplicated, embracing joy of living—was a feeling that he brought to strangers he met in the course of his travels or who met him through the media. It was a sense, a feeling that people recognized in Orville and cherished, and so they cherished him.

And people did cherish Orville Redenbacher, and not only his family and friends and those who benefited from his charitable contributions and activities, but also people who only gathered a feeling about the man through their televisions.

"He's an inspiring man," Gary once said. "He inspires me, he inspires everyone whom he comes across. And, of course, he is a tremendous success, but I think part of that success is because of the man he is."

Through it all, concluded Gary, "He's still Grandpa."

And Orville kept going. Though he had long before given up involvement in the day-to-day operations of his business, he never really slowed down either. As he said of his lifetime contract with Hunt-Wesson, "When I die, I get to quit."

And Orville Redenbacher's Gourmet popping corn continued to grow in popularity along with its founder and guiding spirit. An example, and a powerful one at that: Hunt-Wesson signed a contract with the Walt Disney Company to be the exclusive provider of all the popcorn sold and used at Walt Disney World in Florida and Disneyland in California.

In support of that deal, Orville did a television commercial with his new best friend, Goofy. In the course of the commercial, Goofy holds up a sign, just as Orville is going into his big wind-up— "You'll like it better or my name isn't…"

Goofy unfurls his sign, which read "Orville Ledenracher."

Eternally calm, Orville rights this wrong for the camera. "That's Orville Redenbacher."

Following his eighty-fifth birthday, Orville began to rely more on his grandson Gary in his personal appearances. Though his mind was still sharp as a tack, he was moving more slowly. Together they emerged as a familiar act on the media circuit.

Orville had no problem laughing at himself, even in the silliest way, as he did, along with Gary, on NBC's *Late Night With Conan O'Brien,* October 29, 1993.

The show featured a sketch where Conan's sidekick, Andy, told Conan about a costume he had ordered for Halloween. Conan expressed interest in seeing the costume so Andy left to put it on. Andy exited and then moments later, Orville and Gary walked out together, Gary's arm across his grandfather's shoulder, both men bearing bags of popcorn.

The audience cheered and Orville opened his mouth to speak. However, it was Andy's voice that was heard, as though he was inhabiting some Orville-and-Gary costume. "Hi, Conan. Do you like my costume?"

"Andy?" Conan asked.

"Yeah," mouthed Gary, again with Andy's voice actually doing the talking. "Happy Halloween."

"Not bad," Conan admitted.

"Drop dead, O'Brien," pronounced Andy through Orville's mouth.

The audience howled in delight as Orville and Gary turned and left the set.

An appearance on *You Bet Your Life* earlier in that same year on March 4 provided a forum for demonstrating Orville's impressive mental agility. Bill Cosby was the host and he introduced his guests on this "special" show, which was dedicated to sons who followed in the footsteps of their fathers and grandfathers.

Orville and Gary stepped onto the stage to tremendous applause from the unusually large studio audience.

"Quite a crowd," noted Orville.

"Yeah," said Bill. "You're used to working in front of a crowd this size?"

"Not quite," replied Orville.

"You were born where?" asked Bill.

"Brazil," Orville said.

"Brazil?" repeated Bill.

"Indiana," said Orville.

The crowd laughed and Bill Cosby's face contorted into one of his trademarked funny frowns.

"Gotta get used to it," said Gary. "He'll keep doing that to you."

"He keeps dropping it and sucking you in," Bill said. "Now, you're Gary—Redenbacher—Fish."

"Gary—Fish—Redenbacher," said Gary.

"Oh," Bill said. "Why is there no father between you?"

"My mother is his daughter," Gary explained.

"I had three daughters, no sons," said Orville.

"Ah," Bill said. "Okay. Now, this popcorn business of yours… "

"Real corny," Orville said quickly, garnering a laugh from the crowd.

"What's so special about what you did with the corn?" asked Bill.

"Probably the most special thing is that I put my picture on the jar," Orville said. "Makes it different from everyone else."

Now Orville had the audience in the palm of his hand and Bill turned to face the studio.

"Just one second," he barked in mock annoyance. "Now, he's not that funny! I guess you people think you're going to get some free popcorn."

That did it. The assemblage roared its approval.

"You've got fourteen types of popcorn," Bill said over the din.

"Sounds about right," responded Gary. "We're always doing something new."

"Now, who's the one doing things to the popcorn?" inquired Bill.

"Spent all my life," Orville said, "fifty-one years, working with the sex life of the popcorn plant."

Bill mugged for the camera as the audience laughed.

"I warned you," Gary said.

"You be quiet!" Bill jokingly ordered. "So you made these changes. You had a traditional, just a regular popcorn."

"That's right," Orville said. "And I over-pollinated popcorn."

"What was the first change you made?" asked Bill.

"Started in 1941. Breeding it back on itself. Tassel's the male, the silk's the female...," said Orville.

"Yeah," Bill said.

"...and you do that for ten generations to get a pure line," continued Orville, his voice picking up speed, "and cross those two pure lines and get a single cross, and cross that single cross with another pure line, and you get a three-way cross—that's our seed for the popcorn. It takes about ten years."

"Yeah," Bill said again.

The audience rather tentatively applauded and Bill turned toward the people, with a look of disgust on his face.

"What are you clapping for?" he demanded. "You have no idea what he just said. All you know is that it took ten years."

The people laughed heartily, because Bill was right.

"And that's about how long it took me to understand it," added Gary.

"Fourteen types," Bill said.

"All together," Orville said.

It was time to get down to the ostensible reason they were all gathered together (of course, the real reason was so that Bill Cosby, same as original host Groucho Marx before him, could have some clever repartee with the guests), which was the game the show was built around. The contestants had to answer a series of questions in order to win money.

Bill announced that the Redenbachers were playing to benefit the charitable organization, Habitat For Humanity, and the game began.

The topic was geography, as selected by Orville and Gary.

Question number one, as posed by Bill: "What is the name of the one hundred forty-thousand square mile area in the Atlantic Ocean where some one hundred ships and planes have disappeared over the years?"

"The Bermuda Triangle," Orville instantly replied.

Question two demanded the name of South America's largest country, and it was Gary's turn to deliver the correct response. "Brazil."

The third question asked to which country did Victoria Island, Elsmore Island, and Baffin Island belong. This required a brief consultation between Orville and Gary, and then the reply.

"Canada."

Three for three.

The bonus question really put them over the top in the money stakes. The big question: What country's western border touches Greece, while its eastern border rubs up against Iran?

The Redenbacher boys talked it over and then Orville delivered the news...Turkey.

Right again, naturally, and the team had won a cool $6,910 for a very good cause.

And Orville kept going still, kept making his mark, kept having an impact on our national community. A poll of schoolchildren in St. Paul, Minnesota, revealed that twice as many kids had heard of Orville than had heard of Walter Mondale, former U.S. senator and Democratic presidential nominee—from Minnesota, no less.

As has assuredly been made clear by now, his celebrity never meant all that much to Orville, aside from increased business and a lot of fun. He was so frequently asked for his autograph that he had small stickers printed that read, "I met Orville Redenbacher, The Popcorn King," which he would hand out when asked and personalize by signing, "Orville."

Otherwise, he explained, "it would take me all day to write the whole thing."

But that was all for amusement, part of the performance. Contrast those printed cards with the Coronado phone book. Unlike Hollywood stars, as well as lawyers and doctors and teachers and teenagers and many others, Orville never thought he needed to remove his phone number from the book. His name and address and number remained in the Coronado telephone white pages, as it always had and always would. And every so often somebody, usually a teenager, would call from somewhere in the U.S., asking if this was the real Orville Redenbacher. And Orville would answer, yes, it was, and they would talk awhile.

Most probably about popcorn.

Orville's homespun nature and his incredible success often made for an interesting combination. A moment for another one of those small stories, just because.

On a flight to Cincinnati, a young woman seated in coach was surprised to find the famous popcorn pusher seated beside her. She had no choice but to pose the obvious question.

"Why," she asked, "are you flying coach?"

"When I'm flying for personal reasons," Orville said, referring to those times when he's footing the bill himself, "I go coach. But when I'm on business, I'm a first-class guy."

With an attitude like that, Orville could have been from New York. Of course he wasn't. He was as middle American as they come. He was born on the farm, he worked the land literally from the moment he could walk and carry a sack or bucket, he studied hard in school, he went to college in his home state, he returned to the land armed with education and imagination and endless faith and energy, and he prospered. He married young and happily, he loved his wife and his children, he kept his word to partners and friends and strangers. He spoke his mind to one and all, and stood up for what he believed.

None of that implied that Orville was stuck in the past. His values and ethics were constant, but his mind was always thinking, his intellect always innovating, his instinct always bold.

From beginning to end, Orville was an original, in the best sense of the word.

"Becoming a millionaire was the farthest thing from my mind," Orville said in a speech during the 1980s. "Popcorn was one of my favorite foods and I just wanted to come up with the best-tasting popcorn in the world. Even as a youngster, I tried to make our local 4-H Club's popcorn better. I suppose that my persistence and stubbornness were somehow responsible for what success I've had. I had been told I was looking for a will-o-wisp, to leave well enough alone. What the world needed was anything but a better popcorn. I didn't listen; usually when someone says something like that to me, that something can't be done, that's exactly what I'm going to do.

"Very simply, ours is a brand you can trust. That's why my picture is on every box and jar. Popcorn is fun. You never see anyone in a bad mood eating popcorn."

As related earlier in these pages, Orville once answered a reporter's question about his "philosophy of business" by reading aloud a magazine article he had written in which he talked about following "the classic homespun principles." In short, the sum of these principles, of Orville's philosophy, was to never give up or stand still or be satisfied or forfeit your integrity. Nothing complicated or artful, to be sure, but absolutely, perhaps profoundly, straightforward and clear—and clear-eyed. The essence of this idea, of Orville's idea, was as easy to understand as it was hard to live up to.

"Honestly, that's all there is to it," Orville concluded. "There is no magic formula."

But some people didn't believe him. They thought, they imagined, they insisted, that he must have a formula, a secret, which would explain his boundless vitality and ebullience, his foresight and his success. Again and again, they asked the same question, phrased this way or that.

Another TV reporter, winding up her interview: "How old are you and what's your secret?"

"I'm eighty-three years old," Orville stated in his straightforward manner on that day as he had over and over again. "There is no secret. I eat a lot of popcorn."

Despite the glory and wonder of popcorn, and especially Orville's popcorn, Orville's answer was, for once, not completely forthcoming, though we can understand why.

For even though Orville might not have possessed a secret or a formula, he surely had something that was pure magic.

For, of course, unequivocally, positively, obviously, and enduringly, Orville's magic was Orville himself.

Epilogue:
The Pop Goes On

We have talked about so much and yet so much more remains unsaid. We have touched upon Orville's family, his upbringing, his education, his career, his achievements, his ideas, his hopes.

But that is all right. The point of this book is not to provide an exhaustive account of every fact and facet concerning the life and times of Orville Redenbacher. For though no one would dispute that Orville surely lived an interesting and accomplished life, the thrust of his life was not only about toiling in the laboratory and working in the fields and building a business and running a company. Instead, the thrust of his life was about exploration and experimentation, about emotional reaching and risking, about relishing each achievement and each moment, about loving his family and helping his friends, about being a part of the community and knowing as much about the world as he could learn so as to better contribute and count.

So the point of this modest book is to offer the reader a glimpse into the heart and soul of the man through a review of the arc of his life, an arc that dared to climb straight up toward the sun.

It is inevitable that we concentrated on the big events in Orville's life, especially on the public events. After all, those events, that popcorn, defined him for all the world and for all time. Popcorn is how we know him—popcorn is why we know him.

But there is more, so much more, so many brief anecdotes, so many fleeting stories, so many glimpses into the essential truth and greater reality from his words and deeds.

Such as the time...

Right before going into a meeting on a trip back to Purdue University, Orville stopped at an office and asked the young woman behind the desk if he could leave his briefcase with her for safe-keeping. When he returned to retrieve it, Orville discovered that the woman had locked the case inside her desk. Orville told her such singular care really wasn't necessary for his bag.

The woman replied that such a beautiful briefcase demanded an especially safe place.

"Do you really like it?" Orville asked.

"Oh, yes," she replied.

Without another word, Orville emptied the contents of the case and gave it to her.

Another small story, perhaps, insignificant in the grander sense, but worth repeating nonetheless.

And then another story...

Orville and Corinne led thirty-six men and women on an Indiana Agricultural Group Goodwill delegation through Europe in 1967. As happens on such tours, not every arrangement fell exactly into place. When the group reached a small town north of the Arctic Circle, only thirty-four beds were available in the hotel. So Orville and Corinne took it upon themselves, as the hosts, to sleep in an attic that night.

And we could go on virtually forever with another and another and another story, a lifetime of stories and good deeds and kind words and honors and triumphs, leaving in their wake warm memories and lasting achievements for all who wish to embrace and enjoy.

A Legend Dies

Death came suddenly and unexpectedly to Orville on September 19, 1995, during his eighty-eighth year. Nina had passed away almost four years before, and Orville died alone in his apartment, apparently from a heart attack.

He had previously arranged for his body to be cremated and his ashes scattered over the Pacific Ocean offshore from his Coronado home. No funeral service was held, as per his written instructions. He did not want to cause his family any unnecessary expense, nor engender any undue fuss. Instead, he simply asked his family and friends to enjoy their memories of him as a life to be celebrated and not a death mourned.

Orville was accused on more than one occasion of not being an authentic popcorn pioneer, of actually being an actor.

Orville's reply was always the same. "If I were an actor," he would say, "they'd get somebody much better than me up there."

One more good line from Orville, no doubt, but an impossible proposition. He was the best because Orville was, simply, Orville. He did more than invent a better popcorn, he invented an industry, and added a healthy, fun, delicious component to everyday life. He did all that and he did it as he believed it should be done.

"I try to act like I've always acted, like a farm boy from Indiana."

He succeeded in acting like he always acted, and sometimes that was like a farm boy from Indiana, sometimes that was like a distinguished scientist, sometimes that was like a world-class entrepreneur, sometimes that was like an honored philanthropist, sometimes that was like a loving husband, father, grandfather, great-grandfather, and friend. Orville Redenbacher played many roles in his life, and he played them all well. Perhaps he touched so many people because he embodied what we instinctively, inherently, wish for ourselves and what we value in others.

It is easy for the reality of a person's life to get lost in a mass of images and publicity and advertisements. The reality gives way to the fable.

The same could happen to Orville. He is tailor-made for legend status. Maybe, fifty or one hundred years from now when all that will be left of his legacy is a photo on a package of popcorn—Gourmet popcorn, you can be sure—he will cease to be an American treasure and become an American myth.

And that would be a shame.

Because Orville Redenbacher—thick glasses, bow tie, skinny frame and all—was worth knowing.